DEMONS, DREAMERS,
AND MADMEN
The Defense of Reason in Descartes's Meditations

THE HISTORY OF PHILOSOPHY
SERIES

Under the General Editorship of Harold Weisberg

DEMONS, DREAMERS, AND MADMEN
The Defense of Reason in Descartes's Meditations

HARRY G. FRANKFURT
The Rockefeller University

The Bobbs-Merrill Company, Inc.
Indianapolis • New York

Copyright © 1970 by The Bobbs-Merrill Company, Inc.
Printed in the United States of America
Library of Congress Catalog Card Number: 70-75142
First Printing

FOREWORD

The history of philosophy has long been an important area of philosophical endeavor and even in our "age of analysis" it continues to attract philosophers. Interest in general histories of philosophy may have waned—multivolume general histories are rare and with few exceptions one-volume general histories are basically textbooks—but there is no shortage of articles and books on particular writers, specific periods, and the history of "classic" problems of philosophy. Indeed, the history of philosophy is a steadily growing field.

It is our hope that *The History of Philosophy Series* will stimulate studies in the history of philosophy, not only by those who specialize in this field, but also by those who have primarily analytic concerns but are inclined toward historical investigations. This series seeks to encourage historical study by providing an opportunity for intensive study of a man, his problem, or his period. Moreover, the series will cover a wide range of men and periods, and thus, we hope a contribution to our general knowledge of the history of philosophy will emerge. The individual volumes will not be simply historical narratives. Rather it is expected that critical analysis of a given text or period will provide a further clarification of traditional interpretations, perhaps a new analysis, and a contribution to the understanding of various philosophical problems.

Professor Harry G. Frankfurt's *Demons, Dreamers, and Madmen: The Defense of Reason in Descartes's Meditations* clearly indicates what can be done. Although Descartes's *Meditations* has been studied and restudied by generations of scholars, Professor Frankfurt offers us a fresh analysis and interpretation. Some of his points will be controversial, but his arguments are put forth with rigor and originality and his narrative is compelling. The treatment

Foreword

as a whole puts Descartes in an enlightening perspective and shows again the greatness of his work.

Harold Weisberg
General Editor

PREFACE

The scope of this book is very limited. It deals only with the *Meditations* and only with those parts of the *Meditations* that I believe are indispensable to understanding Descartes's attempt to provide a justification of reason. Part One is devoted almost entirely to an exploration of the First Meditation. Part Two deals with those aspects of later Meditations that bear on the interpretation of the epistemological doctrine with which I am primarily concerned. The last chapter of the book offers an hypothesis concerning the relation between the theory of knowledge inherent in the *Meditations* and the controversy over the significance of scientific truth that developed in the seventeenth century between Galileo and the Catholic Church.

I have not attempted to present a comprehensive and balanced account of everything Descartes says about all the topics I discuss. In dealing with certain problems, for example the validation of reason, I have tried only to identify and develop one important and interesting tendency of his thought. I do not wish to be understood as denying that impressive support can be found for interpretations other than my own, which focus on other tendencies.

I am deeply grateful to my friend Norman Kretzmann for his invaluable assistance and for his encouragement. He translated all the quoted passages that were originally written in Latin (the translations from the French are my own). He also read the book in manuscript and made a large number of important suggestions for improving it. He invariably responded to my requests for help without hesitation or reserve. In this matter, as in others, I relied heavily on his friendship and he never failed me.

Preface

I wish to acknowledge my good fortune in having been the beneficiary of the remarkable competence and the cheerful concern of Miss Frances Fine, who prepared the typescript of this book. I also wish to thank the editors of the *Philosophical Review* and of the *American Philosophical Quarterly* for permitting me to include in this book material already published in their journals.

I dedicate this book to my wife, Marilyn, and to my daughter, Katherine Alexandra.

H.G.F.

CONTENTS

Part 1 THE FIRST MEDITATION

1   INTRODUCTION

In the *Theaetetus*, Plato describes thinking as a conversation conducted by the soul with itself.[1] This has sometimes been taken as a reason for admiring his use of the dialogue form. Koyré goes so far, in fact, as to maintain that "the dialogue is the form *par excellence* for philosophic investigation, because thought itself, at least for Plato, is a 'dialogue the soul holds with itself.' "[2] But a dialogue is not a conversation with oneself. It is a conversation with other people. If thinking is indeed internal discourse, then dialogue can hardly be the ideally appropriate literary form in which to convey it. A much more appropriate vehicle is the meditation, in which an author represents the autonomous give and take of his own systematic reflections.

Moral and religious meditations were published before the seventeenth century, but Descartes was the first to use the form in an exclusively metaphysical work.[3] During his lifetime he published three major philosophical books. One of these, *Principles of Philosophy*, was meant as a text for use in the schools, and its form was dictated by this intention. But in the *Discourse on Method* and in the *Meditations*, Descartes was free to write philosophy as he liked. Both books are autobiographical. Like Plato's dialogues, they do not emasculate the philosophical enterprise by severing its connection with the lives of men. Descartes differs from Plato, however, in the way he solves one of the touchiest problems of philosophical writing—to protect the vital individuality of philosophical inquiry without betraying the anonymity of reason.

Plato never enters the dramatic scenes he creates. He may intend

[1] 189e and 263e.
[2] Alexander Koyré, *Discovering Plato* (New York: Columbia University Press, 1945), p. 3*n*.
[3] Étienne Gilson, *Études sur le rôle de la pensée médiévale dans la formation du système cartésien* (Paris: J. Vrin, 1951), pp. 186-187.

to signify by this self-effacement his refusal to use the stage of inquiry for personal display.[4] There is a certain tension, however, between his conception of inquiry and the literary genre he chose. Plato insists that philosophy and rhetoric are antithetical, but his dialogues would have been lifeless if he had rigorously excluded rhetoric from them. If the characters in a dialogue are to appear as persons, and not merely as devices for punctuating the text, rhetorical elements must naturally intrude into their discourse just as they do into the conversations of real people.

Descartes avoids this difficulty by declining to place his inquiry within a social context. He does his thinking in private, and no one appears in his *Meditations* but himself. To be sure, his style is personal and sometimes even intimate. But while he writes autobiography, the story he tells is of his efforts to escape the limits of the merely personal and to find his generic identity as a rational creature. Whatever actually may have been his motives in publishing the *Discourse* anonymously, philosophically it was appropriate for him to do so. His attitude toward philosophy is nicely implicit in the paradox of an anonymous autobiography, which serves to reveal a man but which treats the man's identity as irrelevant.

Religious meditations are characteristically accounts of a person seeking salvation, who begins in the darkness of sin and who is led through a conversion to spiritual illumination. While the purpose of such writing is to instruct and initiate others, the method is not essentially didactic. The author strives to teach more by example than by precept. In a broad way the *Meditations* is a work of this sort: Descartes's aim is to guide the reader to intellectual salvation by recounting his own discovery of reason and his escape thereby from the benighted reliance on his senses, which had formerly entrapped him in uncertainty and error.

In reading the First Meditation it is essential to understand that while Descartes speaks in the first person, the identity he adopts as he addresses the reader is not quite his own. Students of Descartes often fail to take into account the somewhat fictitious point of view from which he approaches his subject, and this frequently leads to serious misunderstanding. As he begins the *Meditations*, Descartes's stance is not that of an accomplished scholar who has already developed the subtle and profound philosophical position set forth in that work. Instead, he affects a point of view he has long

[4] See Ludwig Edelstein, "Platonic *Anonymity*," *American Journal of Philology*, LXXXIII (1962), 1-22.

since outgrown—that of someone who is philosophically unsophisticated and who has always been guided more or less unreflectively in his opinions by common sense.

This is not very surprising, of course, in view of the autobiographical nature of his book. Descartes's meditations occurred years before he wrote the *Meditations*, and the First Meditation represents an early stage of his own philosophical thinking. He makes this quite explicit in the *Conversation with Burman*, where he explains that in the First Meditation he is attempting to represent "a man who is first beginning to philosophize," and where he discusses some of the limitations by which the perspective and understanding of such a person are bound.[5] The lack of sophistication that Descartes affects consists essentially in a failure to appreciate the radical distinction between the senses and reason. Thus it concerns doctrine, not talent, and it is by no means inconsistent with the resourcefulness and ingenuity that Descartes displays in the First Meditation. The talent available to him as he starts his inquiry is his own. It is only the assumptions that govern his initial steps that are naïve and philosophically crude.

This point is also implicit in the method Descartes employs to present his ideas in the *Meditations*. He describes this method in a well-known passage near the end of his Reply to the Second Objections. There he distinguishes between what he calls the "analytic" and the "synthetic" methods of proof, and he observes that "in my *Meditations* I have followed analysis alone, which is the true and best way of teaching."[6] When the synthetic method is used, a system of thought is formally arranged in deductive order: definitions, axioms, and postulates are neatly laid out, as in a geometry textbook, and each theorem is exhibited as conclusively demonstrable from these materials. But there is no inkling of how the materials were arrived at or of how the various theorems were found to be derivable from them. The work of discovery and creation is ignored, taken entirely for granted, and attention is directed exclusively to the certification of its results.

[5] Charles Adam, ed., *Entretien avec Burman* (Paris: Boivin, 1937), p. 64; Charles Adam and Paul Tannery, *Oeuvres de Descartes* (Paris: L. Cerf, 1897–1913), Vol. VII, p. 156, ll. 3-5. I will hereafter refer to the Adam and Tannery edition as "AT." The volume will appear in roman numeral, the page number will follow in arabic, throughout.

[6] AT VII, 156, ll. 21-23. E. S. Haldane and G. R. T. Ross, *The Philosophical Works of Descartes* (New York: Dover, 1955), Vol. II, p. 49. I will hereafter refer to the Haldane and Ross edition as "HR."

Descartes acknowledges the suitability of this method for the exposition of a subject like geometry, where the primary notions involved in the proofs "are readily granted by all."[7] He regards it as quite unsuitable in a work devoted to metaphysics, however, even though he is convinced that the primary notions of metaphysical discourse are ultimately more intelligible than those of geometry. For while the concepts he finds basic in metaphysics are inherently very clear, they are discordant with the preconceptions "to which we have since our earliest years been accustomed."[8] If they are advanced abruptly, therefore, they are quite likely to be rejected as inappropriate or implausible. It is accordingly most desirable to present them in such a way that the reader can appreciate their significance and recognize their priority.

This happens when the exposition is according to the analytic method, which "shows the true way by which a thing was methodically discovered."[9] Analytic accounts are designed not merely to evoke agreement but to facilitate insight; the author invites his readers to reproduce the fruitful processes of his own mind. He guides them to construct or to discover for themselves the concepts and conclusions which, by the synthetic method, would be handed to them ready-made. For this reason an appropriate use of the analytic method requires a relatively unsophisticated starting point. The reader cannot be supposed to possess already the fundamental concepts of the subject at issue, or to be from the start in a position to grasp the truths that the inquiry is supposed to attain.

Descartes's method of exposition in the *Meditations* obliges him to show scrupulous respect for the philosophical naïvete of his intended reader. As he develops his argument he must not require either the use or the understanding of materials that the text has not already provided and that could be acquired legitimately only through philosophical investigations the reader cannot be assumed to have completed. He must take no step for which he has failed to make suitable preparation; at no stage of the work may he presume any greater philosophical progress than he himself has led his reader to achieve.

Descartes was of course fully aware of this. He insists that he "certainly tried to follow that order most strictly" in the *Meditations;* he "put forward first [those things] that must be known

---

[7] HR II, 49; AT VII, 156, ll. 29-30.
[8] HR II, 50; AT VII, 157, ll. 11-12.
[9] HR II, 48; AT VII, 155, ll. 23-24.

without any help from the things that follow, and all the rest are then arranged in such a way that they are demonstrated solely on the basis of things preceding them."[10] Now this provides a valuable principle for use in interpreting the *Meditations*. For it justifies presuming that there is an error in any interpretation according to which Descartes is required to rely at a given point upon philosophical material not already developed at some earlier stage in his presentation.

Now one of Descartes's most provocative doctrines does not appear in the *Meditations* at all. In a number of his letters he maintains that what God can do is not limited by the laws of logic, and that these laws are, in fact, subject to the divine will. "The truths of mathematics," he writes to Mersenne,

> *were established by God and entirely depend on Him, as much as do all other creatures. To say that these truths are independent of Him is, in effect, to speak of God as a Jupiter or Saturn and to subject Him to the Styx and to the Fates. . . . You will be told that if God established these truths He would be able to change them, as a king does his laws; to which it is necessary to reply that this is correct. . . .*"[11]

In another letter, to Mesland, Descartes says: "the power of God can have no limits. . . . God cannot have been determined to make it true that contradictions cannot be together, and consequently He could have done the contrary."[12] There can be little doubt that Descartes actually held this remarkable doctrine. But he never sets it forth in the *Meditations*, perhaps because he feared it would disturb the theologians whose support or toleration he was anxious to enjoy. It would therefore be quite improper to interpret the philosophical position he develops in the *Meditations* in such a way that his views concerning the dependence of the "eternal verities" on the will of God play an essential role in it.

In view of Descartes's emphasis on the importance of order in the *Meditations*, no advice could be worse than that given by Prichard. After observing that Descartes's book is "extraordinarily unequal" and that "some parts . . . deal with what is important and very much to the point" while others are "very artificial and unconvincing," Prichard suggests that

> *the proper attitude for the reader and the commentator is to*

---

[10] HR II, 48; AT VII, 155, ll. 11-14.
[11] Letter to Mersenne, 15 April 1630; AT I, 145, ll. 7-13; 145, l. 28—146, l. 1.
[12] Letter to Mesland, 2 May 1644; AT IV, 110.

concentrate attention on what seem the important parts and to bother very little about the rest. For that reason I shall in fact consider closely certain portions which seem to me central and almost ignore the rest, and I would suggest that you should do the same in reading him.[13]

Descartes would not have been surprised by this attitude; in the Preface to the *Meditations*, in fact, he anticipates being read more or less as Prichard suggests. But he warns there that "those who do not care to comprehend the order and connections of my reasonings and who are out only to prattle about isolated passages, as many are accustomed to do, will not receive much profit from reading this essay."[14] If his account of his thought is viewed as forming a mere collection of philosophical atoms—a compendium into which one may plausibly dip at any point—the result will often be a failure to grasp what he wishes to convey.

In the First Meditation Descartes defines the philosophical enterprise he proposes to undertake; he also sketches and illustrates the procedure by which he intends to carry it out. Without a thorough comprehension of what goes on in this Meditation, it is not possible to understand his conception of the tasks of metaphysics or to evaluate intelligently his solutions to the problems he considers in his book. This comprehension may seem easy to come by. After all, the First Meditation has a reputation for lucidity and its arguments are very familiar. In fact, however, the Meditation is far from fully accessible to a casual reading and important aspects of it are very often misunderstood.

Descartes himself remarks of the *Meditations* as a whole that "on many things it often scarcely touches, since they are obvious to anyone who attends sufficiently to them."[15] But it is more prudent to take this statement as a warning than as a reassurance, particularly in view of Descartes's admonition that "if even the very least thing put forward is not noted, the necessity of the conclusions fails to appear."[16] Because of its basic importance, and because of the rather deceptive clarity inclining many readers to overlook its complexities, the First Meditation needs to be examined with special care.

My aim in Part One of this book is to give an account of the views

[13] H. A. Prichard, *Knowledge and Perception* (Oxford: Clarendon Press, 1950), p. 72.
[14] HR I, 139; AT VII, 9, l. 28—10, l. 2.
[15] HR II, 49; AT VII, 156, ll. 3-5.
[16] HR II, 48-49; AT VII, 156, ll. 1-3.

Descartes develops in the First Meditation and of the arguments by which he supports them. When he says or does something that seems questionable, I shall sometimes attempt to show that his statement or his procedure is more plausible than it looks. Descartes's brilliance is at times too hasty and impatient; there are gaps in his exposition that he neglected or disdained to fill. Especially when his failures seem most blatant and damaging, I shall endeavor —whenever, at least, I can see how—to offer saving explanations which he himself might reasonably have provided. Whether these explanations actually succeed in saving him from criticism is, of course, another matter.

In general I shall be less concerned with exploring and evaluating the details of Descartes's views for their own sakes than with clarifying the structure of the inquiry he conducts in the First Meditation. I have an ulterior purpose in this. Part Two of this book is largely devoted to elaborating an interpretation of Descartes's discovery and validation of reason. In seeking to understand the nature of the question that he found it necessary to ask about reason, and the answer to it that he thought it possible to give, I have found it useful to recognize that in the First Meditation he raises a question of the same sort about the senses and tries (unsuccessfully, of course) to provide the same sort of answer to it. This parallelism between his discussions of the senses and of reason is, indeed, part of the evidence for the thesis about the latter that I develop in Part Two. The fact that Descartes sees his problem in the First Meditation in a certain way increases, I believe, the plausibility of my claim that he sees the similar problem that he faces later in the *Meditations* in a similar way. It is therefore important for my argument in Part Two, though perhaps not decisive, that I make clear just what goes on in the First Meditation.

Part One presupposes that the reader is familiar with the First Meditation. Here, then, is a translation of it.

FIRST MEDITATION
CONCERNING THOSE THINGS THAT CAN BE CALLED INTO DOUBT

It is now several years since I observed how many false things I accepted as true early in my life, and how dubious all those things are that I afterwards built upon them; and, therefore, that everything must be thoroughly overthrown for once in my life and begun anew from the first foundations, if I want ever to establish anything solid and permanent in the sciences. But the task seemed enormous, and I awaited a time of life so mature that no time better suited for undertaking such studies would follow. On that account I have delayed so long that from now on I would be at fault if I were to use up in deliberating the time left for acting. Today, then, I have opportunely freed my mind from all cares and arranged a period of assured leisure for myself. I am quite alone. At last I shall have time to devote myself seriously and freely to this general overthrow of my opinions.

For this purpose, however, it will not be necessary for me to show that all my opinions are false—which, very likely, I could never manage to do. But reason already persuades me that assent must be withheld no less scrupulously from things that are not entirely certain and indubitable [indubitata] *than from things that are plainly false. For the rejection of all my opinions, therefore, it will be enough if I discover in each one of them some reason for doubting. And they need not be gone over one by one for that purpose— that would be an endless task. But when the foundations have been undermined, whatever has been built up upon them will collapse of itself. Hence I shall immediately attack the very principles on which everything I once believed depended.*

Unquestionably, whatever I have accepted until now as true in the highest degree I have received either from the senses or through the senses. From time to time, however, I have caught them deceiving, and it is prudent never to trust entirely in those who have cheated us even once.

But it may be that even though the senses do deceive us from time to time regarding things that are very small or too far away, there are nevertheless many other things regarding which one plainly cannot doubt even though they are derived from those same senses: for example, that I am now here, sitting by a fire, dressed in a winter cloak, touching this paper with my hands, and the like. Indeed, by what reasoning could it be denied that these very hands and this whole body of mine exist? Unless perhaps I were to consider myself to be like certain madmen, whose brains are being broken down by a vapor from the black bile, a vapor so perverse that they calmly assert that they are kings (when they are in extreme poverty), or that they are dressed in purple (when they are naked), or that they have earthenware heads or that they are nothing but pumpkins, or blown out of glass. But they are madmen, and I should seem no less mad if I were to take them in any way as a model for myself.

How eminently reasonable! As if I were not a man who is used to sleeping at night and to experiencing in dreams all those very things—or, from time to time, things even less probable than the ones such madmen experience while they are awake. Indeed, how often am I persuaded during my nightly rest of these familiar things —that I am here, wearing a cloak, sitting by a fire—although I lie undressed between the sheets.

But now, at any rate, I am surely looking at this paper with wakeful eyes, this head that I am shaking is not asleep, I am deliberately and knowingly extending this hand, and I am having feelings. A sleeping man would not have such distinct experiences.

As if I did not recall having been deluded at other times by similar thoughts in dreams! Now that I think over these matters more attentively, I see so plainly that one can never by any certain indications distinguish being awake from dreaming that I am amazed. And this very amazement almost confirms the conjecture that I am dreaming.

Well then, suppose that we are dreaming, and that these things— that we open our eyes, move our head, extend our hands—are not true, and even that we do not actually have hands or a body. Even so it surely must be acknowledged that things seen during sleep are like painted representations, which could not be formed except in the likeness of truly real things. And so it must be acknowledged that at least things of these kinds—eyes, head, hands, and the whole body —exist as real things, not imaginary, but true. For as a matter of fact even when painters themselves strive to depict sirens and satyrs with the most extraordinary forms, they cannot provide them with natures that are novel in every respect, but can only mix together the parts of different animals. Or even if they should happen to think up something so novel that nothing at all like it had been seen, and thus something that is entirely fictitious and false, at least the colors out of which they compose it would surely have to be true colors. And for the same reason, even if things of these kinds—eyes, head, hands, and the like—could be imaginary, still it must be acknowledged that certain other simpler and more universal things are true and that out of these "true colors" are formed all the true and the false representations of real things in our thought. These seem to be of that sort: corporeal nature in general and its extension, the shape of extended things, the quantity (or the size and number) of those things, the place in which they exist, the time through which they last, and the like.

11

In the light of these considerations, perhaps we are right to con-clude that physics, astronomy, medicine, and all other disciplines that depend on a consideration of composite things are indeed doubtful; and that arithmetic, geometry, and others of that sort, which treat only of the simplest and most general things and scarcely care whether those things are in nature or not, contain something certain and indubitable [indubitati]. *For whether I am awake or asleep, two and three joined together are five, and a square does not have more than four sides. And it seems that it cannot be the case that truths so evident should incur any suspicion of falsity.*

Nevertheless there is a certain opinion, long established in my mind, that there is a God who can do everything and by whom I have been created as I am. Now how do I know he has not brought it about that there is no earth at all, no sky, no extended thing, no shape, no size, no place, and that all these things should nevertheless seem to me to exist just as they do now? And what is more, just as I sometimes judge that others are mistaken about the very things that they consider themselves to know most perfectly, how do I know that God has not brought it about that I am mistaken every time I add two and three together or count the sides of a square or [do something even simpler], *if anything simpler can be imagined?*

And yet, perhaps God willed that I should not be deceived in that fashion, for he is said to be supremely good. But if it should be inconsistent with his goodness to have created me so that I am always mistaken, it would seem no less foreign to his goodness to allow that I should be sometimes mistaken, which, however, cannot be maintained.

Of course, there may be some who prefer to deny so powerful a God rather than to believe that all other things are uncertain. But let us not oppose them, and let us grant that all this regarding God is fictitious. Let them suppose that I have become what I am by fate, or by chance, or by a connected series of things, or in any other way you please. Since it seems to be a kind of imperfection to be mistaken and to err, the less power they ascribe to the author of my origin, the more probable it will be that I am so imperfect that I am always mistaken.

I certainly have no response to these arguments. On the contrary, I am finally forced to acknowledge that of those things I formerly considered to be true there is nothing regarding which it is not legitimate to doubt. And this is not through lack of consideration or frivolity, but for valid and meditated reasons. If I want to find something certain, therefore, assent must be carefully withheld from those things one after another no less than from things obviously false.

But it is not yet enough to have observed these things; I must be careful to bear them in mind. For the familiar opinions come back again and again and dominate my belief, which is tied to them even entirely against my will by long use and the privilege of intimate acquaintance. Nor will I ever get out of the habit of assenting to and trusting in them as long as I take them to be as they really are: doubtful in a way, to be sure (as has just now been shown), but nonetheless highly probable—opinions that it is far more reasonable to believe than to deny.

That is why, in my view, I shall not be acting incorrectly if, with my will plainly set in a contrary direction, I deceive myself and pretend for a while that they are altogether false and imaginary. Then finally, the scales being balanced with prejudices on both sides, no bad habit will any longer twist my judgment away from the right perception of things. For I know that no danger or error will ensue during that time and that my disbelief cannot be overindulged, since I am now committed not to acting but only to knowing.

I will suppose, therefore, not a supremely good God, the source of truth, but some evil spirit who is supremely powerful and cunning and who has expended all his energy in deceiving me. I will suppose that the sky, the air, earth, colors, shapes, sounds, and all external things are nothing but the delusions of dreams by means of which he has set traps for my credulity. I will consider myself as having no hands, no eyes, no flesh, no blood, no senses of any kind, but as thinking falsely that I have all those things. I will remain firmly fixed in this line of thought [meditatio] *and thus, even if it is not in my power to know anything true, still—this* is *in my power—I will at least not assent to anything false. With firm resolution I will be on my guard so that the deceiver, however powerful, however cunning, cannot trick me in any way.*

But this is a laborious undertaking, and a kind of laziness reduces me to the ordinary way of life. Just as a prisoner who happened to be enjoying an imaginary liberty in dreams is afraid to wake up when he later begins to suspect that he is asleep, and readily connives with the agreeable illusions, so I willingly slide back into my old opinions. I dread to be awakened lest my peaceful rest should be succeeded by a laborious wakefulness that would have to be spent not in the light, but in the midst of the inextricable darkness of the difficulties that have just been raised.

2

THE GENERAL OVERTHROW
OF BELIEF

When Hobbes rather derisively characterized the skeptical arguments of the First Meditation as "those old things," Descartes acknowledged without dismay that they are indeed a bit stale. He went on to explain, however, that he had three important reasons for employing them. First, they are necessary in order "that I might prepare the readers' minds for considering intellectual matters and for distinguishing them from corporeal matters." Second, he intends to "respond to these very [reasons for doubting] in the succeeding meditations." And third, the arguments "show how firm the truths are that I put forward afterwards, since they cannot be shaken by those metaphysical doubts."[1]

The second and third of these reasons have to do with the desirability of establishing, early in the *Meditations,* a measure of the power and adequacy of the philosophical alternative to common sense that Descartes develops later in his work. The first reason concerns the importance of making it clear that an alternative is needed. The skeptical excursion of the First Meditation is designed to make this clear by wrecking the thoughtless confidence in sense perception with which common sense is generally content. It is intended to render the philosophical novice to whom Descartes addresses himself, and in whose behalf he speaks, susceptible to an intellectual conversion—a conversion from reliance on the senses to appreciation of the essential role of reason in the acquisition of knowledge.

It is not easy to lead a man away from his natural and comfortable trust in the senses and induce him to commit himself unreservedly to a less palpable and less familiar source of knowledge. It cannot be done, Descartes believes, merely by proving to him that a com-

[1] For Descartes's exchange with Hobbes, see HR II, 60-61; AT VII, 171, l. 16–172, l. 7.

mitment to reason is reasonable. Long-standing habits have to be overcome, and this is possible only if the necessity of breaking the habits is made vivid and compelling. That is why Descartes wants the First Meditation to be studied conscientiously despite the fact that its arguments are neither especially novel nor particularly complex. The purpose of these arguments is not simply to change the reader's mind, but to shake his will. What the Meditation offers is, as Gilson observes, not so much a theory to be understood as an exercise to be practiced.[2]

Descartes ends the First Meditation doubting all propositions concerning perceptual objects and, indeed, skeptical of the very existence of the material world. The arguments that lead him to this uncertainty, he says, provide "valid and meditated reasons" for his doubts.[3] Yet he seems to contradict this statement when he explains to Hobbes that he offers the arguments "only as if probable" and that he intends in due course to rebut them.[4] In fact, the arguments do not hold up; Descartes shows in subsequent Meditations that the reasons he advances for being skeptical are not such good reasons after all. If they seem "valid" in the First Meditation, they do so only from an inadequate point of view; if they are thoroughly "meditated" there, it is only within the confining limits of common sense.

From the perspective of common sense, which Descartes maintains throughout the First Meditation, it is not possible for him to see in what ways his arguments are faulty or to avoid the skepticism they appear to entail. But this does not deprive the argumentation of the First Meditation of its value, because the point of it is, in effect, to provide a *reductio ad absurdum* of the philosophically naïve position from which Descartes conducts it. It is designed to show that common sense generates difficulties from which it cannot escape, and in this way to make the reader receptive to a more authentic theory of knowledge. I intend, in later chapters, to give a fuller account of the common-sense doctrine whose viability Descartes is anxious to undermine, and to analyze the series of arguments by means of which he attempts to reduce common sense to absurdity. What I wish to discuss now, however, is the structural

---

[2] "La première méditation n'est plus une théorie à comprendre; c'est une exercice à pratiquer." Étienne Gilson, *Études sur le rôle de la pensée médiévale dans la formation du système cartésien* (Paris: J. Vrin, 1951), p. 186.

[3] Throughout Part One I shall give no citations for passages quoted, like this one, from the First Meditation itself.

[4] HR II, 60-61; AT VII, 171, l. 19.

role of this series of arguments in the general philosophical program to which he dedicates himself at the very outset of the *Meditations*.

There is a passage in the *Discourse on Method* that provides a suggestive background to the seemingly ruthless decision with which Descartes begins the First Meditation:

> *Since we have all been children before being men and since we have necessarily been governed for a long time by our appetites and by our teachers (who have often contradicted one another, and none of whom perhaps always gave us the best counsel), it is almost impossible that our judgments should be as pure or solid as they would have been if we had had complete use of our reason since birth, and had never been guided except by it.*[5]

Men endure a long period of intellectual dependence and passivity before they become fully adult. By the time they learn to employ their rational faculties autonomously, they have been so far corrupted by passion and preconception that they cannot make good and effective use of reason. One way to describe Descartes's response to this problem is to say that he proposes to regain the intellectual innocence of a child while leaving the mature strength of his rational power intact. He envisages for himself a kind of rebirth. Intellectual salvation comes only to the twice-born.

The opening sentences of the First Meditation explain that the first step in his attempt to establish something "solid and permanent in the sciences" is to be no less radical a measure than the "general overthrow of my opinions." Since he has observed that a number of his most fundamental beliefs are false, he decides that all his opinions must be "thoroughly overthrown . . . and begun anew from the first foundations." This proposal has a heroic ring. It has sometimes been ridiculed by critics who imagine that it either requires Descartes to render his mind an impossibly utter and literal blank or commits him to a more extravagant skepticism than any man can genuinely embrace. Both of these interpretations, however, misconstrue the character and import of his decision. Descartes does not propose to make himself into a *tabula rasa*, and the skepticism to which he commits himself is innocuously thin and undisruptive.

Indeed it is inappropriate to describe it as skepticism at all. Consider the example of a mathematician who is, let us say, attempting to construct a system of arithmetic. If he has so far failed or neglected to establish that "2 + 2 = 4" is a theorem of his

[5] HR I, 88; AT VI, 13, ll. 2-12.

system, he will quite properly refuse to assume in his inquiry that the equation is true. This is hardly a matter of skepticism, and it would be inane to argue, as it has been argued occasionally against Descartes, that the mathematician's refusal is insincere or that his project is absurd because it is psychologically impossible for him to cease believing that $2 + 2 = 4$. The mathematician continues, of course, to "believe" the equation, but he does not accord it a place in the system he is developing because it has not yet passed the tests for inclusion. Within the context of his theoretical work in arithmetic, then, he does not yet "believe" that $2 + 2 = 4$. When he undertook his work he "overthrew" all such beliefs in the limited sense that he decided not to take their theoretical credentials for granted.

Descartes's immediate interests in the *Meditations* are, like those of the mathematician, theoretical rather than practical. He insists that "I have distinguished very strictly between the ordinary way of life and the contemplation of truth,"[6] and he points out that in the *Meditations* he is "committed not to acting but only to knowing." Within the limited context created by his intention to develop a system of knowledge, his resolution to overthrow all his opinions requires him neither to replace his mind with a blank nor to cease acting on the basis of his usual convictions. It demands no more of him than a recognition that the slate of his proposed theory is clean because he does not yet know any proposition to have a legitimate place in the system of knowledge he wishes to construct.

This kind of general suspension of assent is a normal and appropriate initial step in any inquiry that purports to be systematically rational. Even philosophers who believe that it is reasonable to take certain things for granted must in good conscience provide some argument for this belief, and their slates too are clean until they have provided it. Descartes's decision to overthrow all his beliefs is, then, less portentous than it may sound. Far from being heroic, it is simply routine.

But how does he propose to implement his decision? If the decision requires him simply to defer accepting any proposition until he has shown that it satisfies the appropriate criteria, then it would seem that he should be able to carry the decision out in a rather straightforward way. A person can at any time overthrow all his beliefs and start again from scratch, in the relevant sense, merely by resolving that from then on he will deny each proposition a place

---

[6] HR II, 44; AT VII, 149, ll. 4-5.

in his system so long as he has not established that it is acceptable. Making this resolution *is* the act of overthrowing his beliefs. No further steps appear to be required.

This is, in fact, just how Descartes himself explains what his decision calls upon him to do:

> Since judging or refraining from judgment is an act of the will ... it is evident that it is under our control; for in order to rid oneself of all prejudice, one need do nothing but resolve to affirm or deny none of the matters one has previously affirmed or denied, except after a fresh examination. But yet one does not on that account cease to retain all these same notions in his memory.[7]

The provisional suspension of judgment to which Descartes commits himself results directly from a decision or an act of will. A person suspends judgment merely by resolving that his judgments are suspended.

In the light of this doctrine, that judgment is under the facile control of the will, it is not difficult to understand Gassendi's complaint that Descartes can accomplish the task of overthrowing his beliefs without any elaborate argumentation and that the skeptical apparatus of the First Meditation is therefore otiose. It would suffice, Gassendi suggests, merely "to indicate simply and in a few words that all you previously knew is uncertain."[8] What Descartes says about the ease with which a person can overthrow his opinions makes Gassendi's point seem very plausible. But Descartes nevertheless rejects it. In his Reply he emphatically denies that it is easy for men "to free themselves from the errors in which, since infancy, they have been steeped."[9] The skeptical arguments of the First Meditation have an essential role, he insists, in the general overthrow of his opinions.

I intend to argue that Descartes's account of this matter is not entirely coherent. But his answer to Gassendi does not really conflict, although it may appear to do so, with his own statement that "in order to rid oneself of all prejudice, one need do nothing but resolve to affirm or deny none of the matters one has previously affirmed or denied, except after a fresh examination." Emptying the mind takes only an uncomplicated act of will. If this act is not to be arbitrary, however, it must be preceded by the development of an argument that justifies it. If it is not to be ephemeral and incon-

---

[7] HR II, 126; AT IX, 204, ll. 7-16.
[8] HR II, 136; AT VII, 257, ll. 26-27.
[9] HR II, 205; AT VII, 348, ll. 18-19.

clusive, it must be followed by a vivid and watchful self-consciousness that sustains its thrust; and argument has a role in providing
and supporting this self-consciousness.

Descartes makes this clear in a paragraph immediately following
the passage just quoted:

> *Nevertheless I have said that there is a difficulty in expelling
> from one's belief everything that has previously been put there.
> This is partly because one needs some reason for doubting before
> determining to do so, which is why I propounded in my First
> Meditation the main reasons for doubting. It is also partly be-
> cause whatever resolution one has made to deny or affirm noth-
> ing, one easily forgets it if he has not impressed it firmly on his
> memory; which is why I desired that it be thought of care-
> fully.*[10]

There is no inconsistency between Descartes's claim that a simple
decision suffices to rid a person of all his prejudices and his assertion
that "one needs some reason for doubting before determining to do
so." But it does seem that Descartes gives a mistaken account of
his procedure when he says that he "propounded the main reasons
for doubting"—that is, the skeptical arguments of the First Meditation—in order to justify the general overthrow of his beliefs. If this
were correct, it would mean that these skeptical arguments play an
essential role in his effort to empty his mind and that they *precede*
the general overthrow of his beliefs. In fact, however, the arguments belong to a later phase of his inquiry. Despite what Descartes
says in the passage I have just quoted, it is not his skeptical arguments that provide him with the reason he needs in order to justify
his decision to suspend all his judgments.

In his Reply to the Seventh Objections, Descartes offers an
analogy in which he compares his own procedure to that of a person
with a basket of apples, who fears that some of the apples are rotten
and who wishes to remove them in order to protect the rest from
spoiling.[11] This person might reasonably proceed, he observes, by
first dumping out all the apples, then examining each of them and
replacing in the basket just those that pass inspection. Descartes
likewise proposes first to empty his mind of all his opinions, and
then to examine his former beliefs in an effort to identify those
whose credentials entitle them to be reinstated. His enterprise involves first the overthrow of his opinions and then a process of

[10] HR II, 126; AT IX, 204, ll. 16-26.
[11] HR II, 282; AT VII, 481, ll. 4-10.

examining and classifying them. Now Descartes speaks of the skeptical arguments of the First Meditation as belonging to the first of these phases, but they actually belong to the second.

The basket-of-apples analogy suggests that emptying one's mind is a rather headlong and indiscriminate affair. The process of examining and evaluating the mind's former contents, on the other hand, plainly requires meticulous discrimination and careful argument. This makes it far more plausible to suppose that Descartes's skeptical arguments have to do with the task of deciding which of his former opinions are worthy of being reinstated than to suppose that they are designed to bring about the general overthrow of his beliefs. These arguments are in the service of his criterion of doubt, by which he proposes to evaluate his opinions, and it would be incongruous for him to adopt this criterion in order to execute his intention to divest himself of *all* his beliefs. For the criterion has no use except to enable him to discriminate between those of his beliefs that are and those that are not to be rejected.

Moreover, if Descartes can suspend a belief only after he has found some argument to justify doubting it, then it is difficult to understand how he can know in advance that an examination of his opinions will lead him to find a reason for doubting each of them. Yet he does open the First Meditation with an unequivocal commitment to overthrow all his opinions. He needs, to be sure, a reason to justify this decision. But the reason he needs is provided quite satisfactorily by his observation in the opening sentence of the First Meditation that his opinions lack a secure foundation. Thus it is a mistake on his part to suggest that it is the skeptical arguments he develops later in the Meditation that establish the legitimacy of his resolution to empty his mind.

The general suspension of judgment with which the First Meditation begins is distinct from the skepticism produced by the arguments Descartes adduces later in the Meditation. It is not necessary to maintain, however, that he is altogether in error when he repeatedly describes those arguments as playing a role in the general overthrow of his beliefs. In addition to the remarks in passages I have already quoted, he indicates in the text of the First Meditation itself that he regards them as having such a role. In the second paragraph of the Meditation he addresses himself to the question of how he is to carry out the general overthrow of his opinions, and he declares that *"for this purpose"* he will have to provide a reason for doubting each of them. What basis is there, then, for his consistently repeated claim that he empties his mind *through* the skeptical arguments of the First Meditation, and not as a preliminary to them?

An answer is suggested by a statement I have already quoted from his Reply to the Seventh Objections: "whatever resolution one has made to deny or affirm nothing, one easily forgets it if he has not impressed it firmly on his memory." This statement suggests an interpretation based on the distinction between ridding oneself of a belief and insuring that one remains rid of it. Even if he can empty his mind by making a decision, Descartes needs to do more than this in order to keep his judgments effectively suspended. Although he believes he can overthrow all his opinions by an act of will at the very outset of his enterprise, he also regards the skeptical arguments of the First Meditation as essential in overcoming the weight of his long-held prejudices and in preventing them from exerting an illicit influence in the reconstruction of the sciences that he proposes to undertake.

Overthrowing one's beliefs is, in one respect at least, like giving up smoking. Suppose that at noon on a given day a man puts out a cigarette and announces in all sincerity that he will never smoke again. Has he given up smoking? It would be something of a joke to pretend that he had done so if, as things turn out, he takes another cigarette a few minutes later and from then on smokes as heavily as before. In that case it would be more appropriate to say merely that beginning at noon he had made a brief effort to give up smoking. If he does succeed in going without tobacco for a considerable period of time, on the other hand, it would undeniably be correct to say that he had given up smoking at noon on the day in question. It is not very difficult to decide to stop smoking; it requires only an act of will. And making the decision may be tantamount to giving up smoking, but *only if the decision is subsequently adhered to.*

There is no need, then, to maintain categorically either that Descartes empties his mind before he presents his skeptical arguments or that he introduces these arguments in order to accomplish the overthrow of his beliefs. When a person makes the resolution that rids his mind of all his opinions, his situation is like that of the smoker who decides to give up his habit: it remains to be seen whether the resolution is actually tantamount to bringing about the intended result. Descartes makes his resolution before he begins to review and criticize his beliefs; he overthrows his opinions, in this sense, at the very start of his meditations. From that point on he is committed to conducting his inquiry without assuming any of the beliefs he has overthrown. His resolution is not adequately reinforced or confirmed, however, until he has provided himself with reasons for doubting the overthrown beliefs. In this sense, his effort to empty his mind is not complete until, at the end of the First Meditation, he has developed arguments that systematically undermine his former opinions.

Up to a point, then, it is possible to explain how Descartes can ascribe to his skeptical arguments an essential role in the overthrow of his beliefs without at the same time denying that there is a sense in which the overthrow takes place before the arguments are introduced. But there is no way, so far as I can see, to reconcile all the relevant data concerning the relation between his general overthrow of his beliefs and the skeptical arguments of the First Meditation. In particular, it is impossible to escape the conclusion that Descartes is in error when he says that there is a difficulty in overthrowing all one's beliefs "partly because one needs some reason for doubting *before* determining to do so, *which is why* I propounded in my First Meditation the main reasons for doubting."[12] This statement is quite unequivocal and decisive. Descartes regards his skeptical arguments as *preceding* the general overthrow of his beliefs that is accomplished by his decision to empty his mind, and not as serving only to reinforce or to confirm their overthrow. But this is a mistake on his part. He tends to confuse the first and second phases of his program, and at times he speaks incorrectly as though the skeptical arguments precede the overthrow of his beliefs.

[12] Italics mine.

3

THE CRITERION
OF DOUBT

A person might decide to suspend all his judgments, and to make an entirely fresh start in developing and organizing his beliefs, solely in order to improve his understanding of the logical or epistemological relations among them. Many attempts at systematization in mathematics and in other branches of knowledge originate in this kind of interest, without involving any doubts about the truth of the propositions in question. Now a desire to develop a systematic body of beliefs is certainly part of what leads Descartes to begin his meditations by emptying his mind. But it does not entirely account for his decision to proceed as he does. His resolution to empty his mind arises explicitly out of his observation that some of the judgments upon which he has based his opinions are false; it does not arise just out of uncertainty about the ways in which his opinions are related to one another. Although he is very much concerned with problems of order, it is not merely the order of his beliefs that he wishes to explore.

Descartes does not formulate, at the beginning of the First Meditation, either a conception of the nature of truth or a general criterion for distinguishing between the true and the false. He gives no examples of the "many false things I accepted as true early in my life," and he makes no effort to explain how he discovered that they are false. What he says is quite compatible, in fact, with the supposition that he has no very definite ideas as to which of his early judgments are false and which are true. Moreover, since he offers no theory of truth, it is not even apparent whether he has any general view of the difference between a true judgment and a false one.

It is only natural, of course, that Descartes should begin his inquiry without supposing that he has a general criterion of truth and falsity. A good part of his work in the *Meditations* is devoted, after all, to considering the reliability of various kinds of evidence —that is, to his attempting to establish a trustworthy criterion of true belief. It would hardly make sense for him to act as though he were equipped from the very start with the criterion his investigation is designed to provide.

Descartes says quite plainly at the outset of the First Meditation that he knows he has made mistakes, and this may suggest that he must have at least a criterion of falsity. His recognition that he has made mistakes does not, however, imply that he can in general identify false beliefs. In order to discover that the set of his opinions includes some that are false, he does not need a criterion that would enable him to identify any false proposition as false; he needs only to know a necessary condition for the joint truth of propositions. If, for example, he knows that a set of propositions must be logically consistent if its members are to be jointly true, then he can conclude of a set that fails to satisfy this condition that it has at least one false member. But this obviously does not put him in a position to pick out the false member or members of the set.

The question of whether Descartes starts out with some more or less specific conception of the nature of truth is more complicated. This is partly because it is not entirely clear to what extent he is actually concerned with the truth and falsity of the beliefs he proposes to consider. He expresses an interest in truth and falsity in the opening sentence of the *Meditations*, to be sure, but it very soon begins to appear that his interest in certain other characteristics of beliefs is more direct and immediate than his interest in their truth-values.

This appears, for example, in the fact that while his discovery that some of his early opinions are false clearly troubles him, he says that it troubles him essentially because it renders the judgments he has based upon those opinions *doubtful*. Moreover, when he explains that he wishes to build a new structure of knowledge from the foundations, he does not justify his proposal by saying that he hopes to arrive at a set of uniformly true beliefs. He explicitly asserts that he wishes to establish beliefs that will be *solid* and *permanent*. It is not obvious that these characteristics, which concern the immunity of a belief to revision, are tantamount to truth. Finally, when he sets out to examine his former opinions he does not identify his aim as being to discriminate between those that are true and those that are false. He says that he wants to determine which of his opinions "are entirely certain and indubitable" and which have in them "some reason for doubting."

As the First Meditation gets under way, then, Descartes's concern apparently shifts from considerations of truth and falsity to those of certainty and doubt. It is somewhat difficult to evaluate the significance of this shift, primarily because it is not very clear how Descartes construes the relation between his conceptions of truth and falsity on the one hand and his conceptions of certainty and doubtfulness on the other. According to what is probably the most common view of the matter—a view usually taken more or less for granted—his conception of certainty is built upon some version of the correspondence theory of truth. When he seeks certainty, on this account, he is after beliefs whose correspondence with reality is certain; and when he asks whether what is indubitable is true, his question concerns whether beliefs that cannot be doubted correspond with reality.

My own interpretation involves a rather different way of understanding him. Although I agree that he sometimes conceives truth and falsity in terms of correspondence, I do not believe that this conception plays a very important role in his treatment of the epistemological problems that concern him most. Descartes seems willing to recognize and to make limited use of a notion of absolute truth, which may be explicated in terms of correspondence. But this absolute truth is not what interests him. I am inclined to take more seriously than do most commentators the following passage, in which he denies that the truth he seeks consists in the correspondence of a belief to reality:

> *What is it to us if someone should perhaps imagine that the very thing of whose truth we have been so firmly persuaded appears false to God or to an angel, and that as a consequence it is false, speaking absolutely? What do we care about this absolute falsity, since we by no means believe in it or even have the least suspicion of it? For we are supposing a persuasion so firm that it can in no way be removed—a persuasion, therefore, that is exactly the same as the most perfect certainty.*[1]

Descartes's most basic and insistent preoccupation is with certainty itself, and he tends to be rather indifferent to the question of whether the certain corresponds or fails to correspond with the real.

While he acknowledges that there is a legitimate conception of truth in which the notion of correspondence is central, Descartes himself makes use of another conception of truth altogether. In fact,

---

[1] Reply to the Second Objections, HR II, 41; AT VII, 145, ll. 1-9.

25

he reverses the more usual order of things in which the notion of certainty is derivative from that of truth. Certainty is his fundamental epistemological concept, and he defines truth in terms of it. Now certainty is for him essentially a matter of the coherence of evidence. It is a coherence theory of truth, accordingly, which most authentically expresses the standards and goals of his inquiry.

I shall discuss these matters more systematically in due course. For the present, however, I am dealing with the early passages of the First Meditation, and in those passages Descartes is concerned mainly with the distinction between the certain and the doubtful. It is in terms of this distinction, rather than in terms of the distinction between true and false, that he undertakes to decide what to believe. Leaving temporarily to one side the question of how the two distinctions are related, I propose to consider the significance and the validity of the criterion of certainty and doubtfulness that he sets out to employ.

Descartes himself offers only the following rather abrupt explanation of his criterion:

> But reason already persuades me that assent must be withheld no less scrupulously from things that are not entirely certain and indubitable than from things that are plainly false. For the rejection of all my opinions, therefore, it will be enough if I discover in each one of them some reason for doubting.

He neither elucidates nor defends this assertion. He gives no account of the reasoning by which he was persuaded to withhold his assent from the uncertain, and he does not explain what is to count as a reason for doubting. But these deficiencies in his discussion can to some extent be repaired.

It is worth noting, to begin with, that what Descartes says does not strictly commit him to rejecting *only* dubitable propositions. He identifies uncertainty as a sufficient condition for the unacceptability of a belief without asserting or implying that it is a necessary condition as well. He says nothing at all, moreover, about which propositions he will accept. If all dubitable propositions are to be rejected, then of course it follows that all acceptable propositions will be indubitable. But this does not provide a criterion for deciding that any proposition is acceptable; it provides only a necessary condition for the acceptability of a belief. As he begins his inquiry in the First Meditation, then, Descartes equips himself with a criterion that enables him to decide only that some propositions are unacceptable. It does not enable him either to decide that a given proposition should be accepted or to conclude that the only propositions unworthy of his assent are those that his criterion leads him to reject.

Descartes has no more than a criterion for the unacceptability of beliefs, and he does no more to justify it than to suggest that it is rationally grounded. But what is the argument by which reason can have persuaded him that his criterion is legitimate? And what can be the authority of its premises for a man whose mind is avowedly empty? These questions are especially pointed, for Descartes's resolution to suspend *all* his judgments appears to leave him with no starting point from which his reasoning can begin.

This appearance is deceptive. Although he must of course respect the resolution by which he has suspended all his opinions, Descartes may quite legitimately reason from a premiss stating the purpose of his inquiry. It is proper for the course of an inquiry to be guided by its goal and, so far as logic is concerned, the goal of the inquiry may be postulated as a matter of free choice. Now Descartes states his purpose in the First Meditation's opening sentence: "I want . . . to establish [something] solid and permanent in the sciences." If reason has already persuaded him of something, despite the fact that his mind is still empty of belief, this postulate must have been the starting point of his argument.

It is rather easy to reconstruct an argument such as the following, by which Descartes could reasonably persuade himself that his criterion is legitimate. A person cannot regard one of his beliefs as altogether solid and permanent if his basis for believing it is compatible with a sufficient basis for giving it up. As long as it is possible for circumstances to arise in which, given the basis he already has for accepting a belief, it would nevertheless be reasonable for him to reject it, then the belief does not provide him with an absolutely secure foundation on which to build. When Descartes considers the aim of his undertaking and concludes that he must assent to nothing except the "entirely certain and indubitable," what is presumably in his mind is that a belief has these characteristics if and only if accepting it involves no risk—no chance at all that additional evidence will ever make it reasonable for him to abandon the belief. This much can be derived merely from the fact that his inquiry is committed to beliefs that are solid and permanent.

Referring to the goal of Descartes's undertaking makes it possible to account for the initial premise of the argument by which he reaches his criterion for sorting his former opinions, but it does not help to explain the authority he evidently accords to reason itself. It does not make it clear how he can be justified in allowing himself to be persuaded by reason at all. Reason itself is not a belief, to be sure, but a faculty. Nevertheless, why is Descartes not obliged, in the general withdrawal of assent to which he commits himself, to withdraw his assent from the opinion that his judgment should be guided by this faculty?

He appears, in fact, to be caught from the beginning of his enterprise in a crippling dilemma. He cannot conduct his inquiry at all unless he relies upon reason. He must acknowledge the claims of logical truths and valid arguments, and he must govern his thinking by the usual standards of relevance and consistency. But at the same time he cannot justify relying upon reason because he has emptied his mind and therefore has nothing with which to construct a justification. If he empties his mind of everything, including his confidence in reason, how can he coherently go on to examine the questions with which he wishes to deal? If, on the other hand, he exempts his belief in the authority of reason from his initial suspension of all judgments, how can he pretend to be engaged in an unqualifiedly radical exploration of the foundations of knowledge? The problem of circularity on which Descartes's enterprise is often alleged to founder arises, in a general way, at this point in the First Meditation.

The key to the solution of this difficulty lies in appreciating the problem with which Descartes intends his inquiry to deal. Even though he does not make his criterion for reasonable doubt explicit, it goes without saying that he is not interested in trifling with baseless cavils or in cultivating a stubbornly dogmatic skepticism. His aim in subjecting his former opinions to critical examination is to determine whether or not there are *reasonable grounds* for doubting them. He wishes to learn what can be doubted "not through lack of consideration or frivolity, but for valid and meditated reasons." The task he sets for himself in the *Meditations* is, in general, to discover how a reasonable man can find a foundation for the sciences. The authority of reason is, accordingly, built into the very conception of his enterprise.

It might be objected that for just this reason Descartes's project is hopeless, since it requires him both to empty his mind altogether and to place his confidence in reason. But an objection of this sort reflects too hasty an estimate of the logic of his inquiry. The fact that his inquiry cannot proceed unless he commits himself to reason does not decisively undermine his resolution to avoid all prejudice. For his commitment to reason is of a kind that does not involve making an assumption that is gratuitously exempted from examination. This is because he does not take it for granted that he will *succeed* in distinguishing some things that it is reasonable for him to doubt and other things that it is reasonable for him to regard as certain. His commitment to reason is not unequivocal or irrevocable but provisional, since he makes no assumption concerning where it will lead him.

Descartes's procedure permits him to acknowledge, in other words, that his enterprise may end in failure. What saves his initial commitment to reason from begging the question is the fact that he starts out with an open mind concerning whether he will actually be able to discover a secure foundation for knowledge in a set of beliefs immune to reasonable doubt. If he should not succeed, his failure would reveal that the confidence in reason with which he begins is unjustified. A decisive failure would, indeed, undermine the entire distinction between the reasonable and the nonreasonable man. Reasonable men are precisely those who are able to distinguish between what it is and what it is not reasonable to doubt— men who make a reasonable distinction between acceptable and unacceptable beliefs. If Descartes's inquiry should show that these distinctions cannot be successfully maintained—that there is no viable distinction between the certain and the doubtful—then the whole conception of a reasonable man would be shown to be empty.

Descartes's assumption that reason is entitled to authority has the status of a working hypothesis whose tenability is itself to be tested by the investigation he undertakes. Viewed in this light, it begs no questions; it does not contravene his resolution to empty his mind. Just as he examines in the First Meditation the assumption that the senses are trustworthy, he considers later in the *Meditations* the assumption that reason is reliable. Since his aim is to discover how (and whether) a reasonable person can find a secure foundation for the sciences, it would be irrelevant for him to begin his inquiry except by adopting a rational norm. But since his adoption of it is provisional and does not prejudge the question of whether using this norm is a viable procedure, he does not arbitrarily settle a question that he is obliged to leave open.

Descartes does very little to explain his conception of the distinction between what is reasonable and what is not. It is possible to explicate the standard he proposes to wield only through analyses of the arguments in which he deploys it. Thus the starting point of his investigation and the identity of his ideal reader cannot become fully clear until his inquiry has progressed beyond its initial stages. Whatever his conception of the reasonable may be, however, Descartes's policy of relying on it is unimpeachable. For his enterprise is essentially an effort to discover whether (and how) someone who relies on it can establish the sciences on solid ground.

4

THE PERCEPTION
OF THE PHYSICAL WORLD

Of the arguments set forth in the First Meditation, those concerning dreams and the demon have attracted the most attention. No one can deny that these two arguments are exceptionally striking and provocative, or that they play central roles in the development of Descartes's metaphysics.

It is unfortunate, however, that comparatively little careful attention has been given to other parts of the discussion that lead to the First Meditation's skeptical outcome. For instance, the reasoning that precedes the dream argument in Descartes's critique of the senses is rarely subjected to close examination. To be sure, this reasoning is not particularly profound, nor is it especially difficult to grasp. Nevertheless it represents Descartes's first application of his "method of doubt" in the *Meditations*, and in the course of it some essential aspects of his metaphysical program become clear for the first time. The reasoning is more complex than it is often taken to be, moreover, and incorrect or misleading accounts of it are frequently given. Finally, a correct understanding of it makes it easier to appreciate the significance of Descartes's concern with dreaming and with the demon.

Descartes wants to examine his former beliefs, but since he cannot hope to inspect each of them individually he decides to consider only certain general principles upon which all of them depend. This is an economical procedure: he may find that the entire membership of a large class of judgments is unacceptable if he discovers grounds for doubting a principle that is used to justify each member of the class. The first general principle he proposes to consider is introduced with the following remark: "whatever I have accepted until now as true in the highest degree I have received either from the senses or through the senses."

The rather obscure phrase "from the senses or through the

senses" expresses, as Descartes explains in the *Conversation with Burman*, a distinction between beliefs derived from personal experience and those based on hearsay.[1] Opinions concerning the colors or shapes of things, for instance, are derived "from the senses" if they derive from actually seeing the relevant colors and shapes. On the other hand, many opinions are acquired from parents, teachers, and other men. These are received by hearsay: "through the senses—that is, through hearing."

When he asserts that all his most assured beliefs are based upon sensory experience, Descartes is speaking from the deliberately naïve point of view adopted in the First Meditation—that of someone who is "first beginning to philosophize." One characteristic of a person of this sort is that he "attends only to those things with which he knows himself to be acquainted." He is convinced, moreover, "as we all are before [we encounter] philosophy," that he has no knowledge except what the senses provide. In Descartes's own view, of course, this conviction is mistaken. Descartes believes that all men have innate knowledge of certain "general principles and axioms—for example, *it is impossible that the same thing should be and not be.*" But the philosophical novice with whose voice he speaks in the First Meditation is as yet unaware that there are non-sensory sources of knowledge.

This man, therefore, pays little attention to common principles or axioms. If he does not neglect them entirely, he assimilates them to sensory experience and considers them only in concrete instances. He is, in this respect, like the unsophisticated geometer whose conceptions are so tied to the drawn figure that he cannot comprehend them in abstraction from an illustration. As for other purely intellectual conceptions—such as those of God or the self— the opinions of the philosophical beginner come to him by hearsay. He knows nothing of such matters directly, for that would require a pure use of reason of which he is still incapable. The common-sense point of view is characterized, then, by a failure to consider abstract principles "separated from matter and from particular instances." It is for this reason, indeed, that Descartes expects his intended reader to find the skeptical arguments of the First Meditation disturbing. A person who is devoted unreflectively to common sense cannot readily detach his mind from its habitual immersion

---

[1] AT V, 146; Charles Adam, ed., *Entretien avec Burman* (Paris: Boivin, 1937), pp. 2-5. All quotations in this and in the next two paragraphs are from this passage.

in sensory experience, and he is therefore unable to perceive the defects in some of the arguments Descartes presents.

A surprisingly common misunderstanding is that Descartes's critique of the senses consists simply in an argument that draws from the fact that the senses are occasionally deceptive the conclusion that they are not to be trusted at all.[2] It is true that Descartes begins with the observation that "from time to time . . . I have caught [the senses] deceiving, and it is prudent never to trust entirely in those who have cheated us even once." But his examination of the senses is not so thin in texture as this. In order to appreciate its relative complexity one must consider all of it, and not just the gambit with which it opens. It is a distortion of Descartes's views to suppose that he regards his remark about prudence as decisive or that he thinks it seriously impugns the reliability of the senses. On the contrary, he recognizes it as preliminary and crude, and he offers it mainly in order to indicate its inadequacy and to improve upon it. The remark is merely introductory to an examination of the trustworthiness of sense perception considerably more sophisticated than many of Descartes's critics have noticed.

Descartes does not merely observe that the senses sometimes deceive and then conclude that beliefs based on their testimony are uniformly unreliable. He rebuts this argument, in fact, immediately after he formulates it. Indeed, throughout the relevant portions of the First Meditation, he seeks to *defend* the senses against objections that he suggests may be raised against them. He attempts to show how confidence in sensory beliefs may reasonably be maintained in the face of these objections by invoking distinctions that deflect their thrust.

What does Descartes have in mind when he speaks of the "principles on which everything I once believed depended"? And what principle is it that he undertakes to examine when he says that all his truest beliefs have come to him from or through the senses? The principles in which he is interested are rules of evidence. When he decides to examine the principles on which his beliefs rest, he is not thinking of a set of logically ultimate propositions or axioms from which his opinions can be deduced. The principles he has in mind are not premises; rather, they define policies to be followed in determining whether or not to accept a belief. During the course of the *Meditations*, he examines principles concerning judgments

---

[2] See, for example, Nicholas Rescher, "The Legitimacy of Doubt," *Review of Metaphysics*, XIII (1959), 230.

based on the senses, judgments based on clear and distinct perception, and "natural beliefs." His question about each of these principles is whether following the policy it defines—i.e., accepting beliefs supported by the kind of evidence the principle certifies—is a reasonable way to attain certainty.

Descartes actually considers in the First Meditation several principles concerning sensory evidence; or, if one prefers to say so, he considers several versions of the same principle. In line with his desire to proceed from an unsophisticated starting point, he begins with the most naïvely uncritical of all policies regarding sense perception; but he quickly shows that this policy is unsatisfactory, and then goes on to discuss a more cautiously conceived alternative. His examination of the senses leading to the dream argument is in fact dialectical: he considers a principle, criticizes it, proposes a revision to cope with the criticism, probes the weaknesses of the revised principle, and so on. Although he does not make any of these principles explicit, it is not difficult to formulate them.

The first objection Descartes raises against the senses is that they are sometimes deceptive. He does not explain how he has found this to be so, but proceeds simply to observe that "it is prudent never to trust entirely" something by which we have once been deceived. Since his point is that it is imprudent to trust the senses *entirely,* the general principle at stake here may be construed as the negation of this, i.e., as asserting uncritically that the senses are *always* reliable. Now the fact that there are cases in which following this principle results in deception does not entail that the senses are never trustworthy or that every sensory judgment must be regarded as uncertain. Moreover, Descartes makes no such inference. He draws only the quite reasonable conclusion that it is unwise to accept sensory testimony indiscriminately. There is a distinction between saying that the senses are not to be trusted entirely (i.e., that it is unwise to accept all sensory judgments) and saying that no sensory judgment is to be trusted entirely (i.e., that every sensory judgment is uncertain). Descartes is occasionally misunderstood to be saying the latter, whereas it is only the former to which he commits himself.

The assertion that the senses are unreliable suggests a question: *unreliable as to what?* If accepting sensory testimony indiscriminately is unwise, just what is it unwise to accept it for? What is involved in "trusting the senses" in the first place? The First Meditation offers no comment on this matter, but clearing it up is not very difficult. In the *Conversation with Burman* Descartes observes, with reference to the First Meditation, that "here it is principally a question of an existing thing—that is, whether it exists."[3] The principle that the senses are always reliable, then, amounts to the claim that whatever is sensed exists as it appears to the senses.

The claim does not concern the existence of objects whose essential nature is to be sensed—i.e., sense-data, or objects constituted by the sensing of them—but rather objects that are independent of being sensed and whose existence is learned by means of the senses. The starting point of Descartes's inquiry is, in other words, a naïvely realistic doctrine according to which sense perception invariably involves the presentation of an independent physical object whose character is just what it seems to be. It is natural, of course, that a person with the intellectual identity of Descartes's inquirer should begin with this principle, which is roughly equivalent to the common-sense dictum that seeing is believing.

If a person is known to lie occasionally, it is not reasonable to accept something *simply* on the ground that he testifies to it. Similarly, once the senses have been discovered to be capable of deception, it is not reasonable to regard a belief as solid or permanent *merely* because it is based on sensory evidence. For it may turn out that the occasion on which the senses provided the evidence for the belief was one on which the senses are deceptive; and then, of course, the belief would have to be abandoned. Despite this, however, it may still be reasonable to regard some sensory beliefs as permanent and indubitable, if occasions on which the senses are absolutely reliable can be distinguished from those on which they are likely to deceive.

Thus after he observes that unrestricted confidence in the senses is unjustified, Descartes attempts to make such a distinction. He tries to distinguish between sensory beliefs that may reasonably be regarded as subject to correction or rejection, and those that may reasonably be accepted as immune to future disturbance. Even a man who lies may be trustworthy concerning some things. In order to keep open the possibility of finding certainty in the senses, Descartes seeks to identify special conditions under which the senses may be trusted without reservation, no matter how unreliable they may be when these conditions do not prevail.

What he says after he rejects the policy of trusting the senses indiscriminately is this:

[3] AT V, 146; *Entretien avec Burman*, pp. 2-5.

though the senses do deceive us from time to time regarding things that are very small or too far away, there are nevertheless many other things regarding which one plainly cannot doubt even though they are derived from those same senses. . . .

He mentions as examples the facts that he is sitting near a fire, wearing a dressing gown, and holding a piece of paper in his hands. A person has reasonable grounds for withholding full confidence from sensory testimony that is gathered when the conditions of perception are in some way unfavorable. But there are other occasions, Descartes suggests, when none of the conditions for perception are unfavorable. The conditions he has in mind are "external" ones—they have to do with the character of the perceived object and with the physical relationships in which it stands to the perceiver. The senses are not to be trusted when their object is very small or very distant. But when circumstances are in no such respect unfavorable, the senses may be relied upon without fear of error.

Descartes proposes a revised principle, accordingly, which may be understood as affirming that the senses are trustworthy whenever they operate under external conditions that are uniformly favorable, that is, whenever there is no basis in the particular external circumstances of their operation for mistrusting them. The objection that overthrew his original version of the principle obviously has no weight against this one. In making that objection, Descartes noted merely that the senses are *sometimes* deceptive. He did not assert that they are ever deceptive when the external conditions for perceiving are ideal.

This second version of the principle, however, is also vulnerable. Even when the external circumstances of perception are ideal, errors may still occur if the perceiver himself is defective. The second principle is satisfied paradigmatically, Descartes suggests, by gross observations of one's own body and of conspicuous objects in its immediate vicinity. Nevertheless, he points out, there are perceivers who are deceived even in matters of this sort. The difficulties of these perceivers do not lie in the external conditions of their observations, for those are ideal; they lie in their brains, which are "broken down by a vapor from the black bile." When external conditions for perceiving are ideal, sensory testimony may still be impugned on the basis of conditions internal to the perceiver.

One might naturally expect Descartes to respond to the example of madmen by considering the possibility of distinguishing between madness and sanity. This would parallel the way in which he copes with the objection raised against the first version of his principle. In dealing with that objection, he distinguished two sorts of perceptions—those made under ideal external conditions and those made under unfavorable ones. Against the doubts now being raised against his revised principle, the most obvious line of defense would consist in making a similar distinction in the case of perceptions occurring under ideal external conditions, that is, in distinguishing between situations in which internal conditions are also ideal and those in which they are not. But in fact Descartes makes no such defense. He simply dismisses the possibility of his own madness with the remark that it would not be reasonable for him to entertain it. Such people are insane, he says of those he has just described, "and I should seem no less mad if I were to take them in any way as a model for myself."

What is the relevance of the fact that there are madmen whose beliefs are often false even when they concern what is perceived under ideal external conditions? Descartes is, of course, attempting to discover whether he can reasonably regard any of his own beliefs as entirely certain. But if he must take into account the possibility that he is mad, then he cannot regard any of his beliefs as indubitable solely because they are based on perceptions occurring under ideal external conditions. The fact that error may arise out of madness suggests that he should be suspicious of all his opinions until he can establish that he is not insane. He does not, however, attempt to establish his sanity, or even to describe a procedure for doing so.

Instead he rather abruptly dismisses the suggestion. He asserts, indeed, that he would be mad to compare himself with the lunatics he has described. Now by what right does he so airily discard the possibility that he is mad? He has resolved to take nothing for granted. Does this not oblige him to suspend even the belief in his own sanity? How can it be proper for him to assume without evidence that he is not mad and to dismiss the possibility of his madness as a basis for uncertainty regarding his sensory beliefs?

Descartes evidently thinks that it is an essential aspect of madness to be unable to distinguish properly between reasonable and unreasonable judgments. The original French translation of the *Meditations*, which he approved, refers to madmen as *"insensées."* This term may mean "those who have lost their reason," a translation which receives some support from Descartes's use of *"bon sens"* to refer to reason in the opening sentence of the *Discourse on Method:* a madman lacks that "good sense," or capacity for rational judgment, which enables other men to distinguish true from false when they employ it correctly. When he claims that it would be unreasonable for him to entertain the possibility that he is insane, then, Descartes is refusing to consider whether he is capable of distinguishing between reasonable and unreasonable judgments.

It seems clear that he has no reasonable alternative and that it would be a mistake to regard his discussion of madness as evidence of a damaging failure to honor his commitment to doubt. The whole point of his critical examination of his former opinions is to determine whether or not there are reasonable grounds for doubting them. If he were to begin by suspending the judgment that he is reasonable, he would be unable ever to reestablish his confidence in his own ability to carry out his task. For if he were to entertain doubts about his own rationality, he would naturally be bound to suspect any reasoning by which he might attempt to establish his sanity. He could not reasonably expect to resolve his doubts (or anything else) in the course of his inquiry.

The task he sets for himself in the *Meditations* is not to discover how a madman can find a foundation for the sciences. A madman cannot do so at all. Unless Descartes supposes himself to be sane he cannot conduct the investigation to which he wishes to devote himself. The question he poses as he undertakes his inquiry, therefore, is this: Assuming that I am a reasonable man, how (if at all) can I attain certainty? His project may fail, and he may for this reason ultimately be led to wonder whether he is not after all incapable of rational discrimination among judgments. His assumption of his own rationality is provisional, like the commitment to reason discussed in the last chapter, and it begs no questions that ought to be left open. Because Descartes's assumption is provisional and heuristic, it does leave the question of his own sanity open. But he cannot raise this question at the start of his inquiry without incoherently undermining the basis of his enterprise.

Now madness is not the only defect with which perceivers may be afflicted. There are many less dramatic abnormalities from which people suffer and which may be responsible for error even in judgments concerning what is perceived under ideal external conditions. But there is no mention in the First Meditation of faulty vision or deafness or the like, and it is natural to wonder why madness is the only defect Descartes considers.

One important way in which madness differs from other defects is in its generality. A person who is deprived of the use of reason is equally incapacitated with regard to all judgments, whereas a sensory defect like color blindness does not interfere with the accuracy of judgments involving the use of faculties other than the defective one. That the inquirer be reasonable is an essential qualification for conducting any inquiry whatever. Normal vision or normal hearing, on the other hand, are prerequisites only for the conduct of inquiries involving visual or auditory data. Normally functioning senses are not at all essential to Descartes in the *Meditations*, since he does not need to make any sensory judgments in the course of investigating whether it is possible to find certainty in the senses.

To be sure, the policy he is considering endorses perceptions that occur under ideal external conditions, and this policy cannot guarantee that judgments will be reliable unless the senses of the perceiver in question are normal. In order to evaluate his own fitness to inquire into sensory matters, a person must naturally determine whether or not his sensory faculties are defective. But Descartes does not discuss this matter because it is not germane to the problem he is addressing. His concern is not with how an individual can decide whether he is personally well-suited for arriving at entirely certain judgments; what he wants to know is whether certainty is attainable at all, even by those who are qualified as well as men can be for its pursuit. He quite rightly takes it for granted, therefore, that the attempt to found certainties on sensory data is to be made by individuals who are not peculiarly unsuited for it by personal handicaps or idiosyncrasies.

He supposes, in other words, that the perceptions in which certainty is to be sought will be those of an ideally qualified perceiver under ideal external conditions. His question is whether it is possible for a reasonable man with normal senses to arrive at sensory judgments that are entirely certain. The third version of the principle he considers may be formulated, accordingly, as follows: whatever is perceived under ideal external conditions by an ideally qualified perceiver certainly exists.

This third version of the principle does not emerge from Descartes's discussion of the second version in as straightforward a manner as the second emerges from his discussion of the first. It may even seem dubious to construe his move to the third version as guided by an encounter with decisive objections against the second. For the only objection he actually raises against the second is the one concerning madness, and this objection is peremptorily dismissed. There is some evidence, however, that his discussion following the passage on madness does have to do with a third version of the principle that the senses are reliable. For one thing, merely personal defects are rather plainly irrelevant to the problem Descartes is considering, and it is plausible that he should revise the second version of his principle so as to cope with idiosyncratic sources of perceptual deception. The revision is a natural and obvious one for him to make. For another, the way in which Descartes introduces his dream argument tends to confirm this interpretation.

Immediately after he dismisses the possibility of his own madness, Descartes takes note of the fact that dreams occur:

> *How eminently reasonable! As if I were not a man who is used to sleeping at night and to experiencing in dreams all those very things—or, from time to time, things even less probable than the ones such madmen experience while they are awake.*

His point is clearly that dreaming is a nonpathological equivalent of madness. Descartes recognizes that it is not appropriate for him to attack the testimony of his senses with the suggestion that he may be abnormal. So he considers an analogue of madness that involves no abnormality.

What he finds interesting about dreams is just that they are phenomena in which the presentation of non-veridical data is normal. The fact that we are asleep while dream data are generated is more or less irrelevant; Descartes could have made his point almost as well in a discussion of daydreaming. (Perhaps not quite as well, because it seems essential to daydreaming that the absorption in fantasy be incomplete; a person daydreams with one eye open, so to speak, and is therefore always aware to some degree that his data are fantasy data. If he were *entirely* immersed in the fantasy data, he *would be* asleep or insane.) Like the abnormal man, the dreamer generates sensory data of his own; he too "lives in his own world." The fact that he perceives non-veridical data is not due, however, to idiosyncrasy or to a defect in his individual constitution. It cannot therefore be dismissed as a fact of merely personal relevance.

It may be asked what right Descartes has, in view of his resolution to doubt everything, to take it for granted that dreams occur at all. Why, moreover, does dreaming require any special consideration? Why not treat dream images simply as special cases of data obtained when the conditions for perception are not ideal? The answers to these questions become clear when the argument of the First Meditation is considered in a correct perspective. Not only does Descartes regard the opinion that he examines throughout his critique of the senses—the opinion that absolutely certain beliefs can be attained through sensory experience alone—as characteristic of unphilosophical men. What must be kept particularly in mind is that he examines this opinion from a deliberately naïve point of view, the point of view of common sense. Descartes's common-sense protagonist is not, of course, stupid or unsubtle; on the contrary, he is capable of defending his convictions with considerable ingenuity. He is not limited by his intellectual ability, but by his assumptions. Only in this respect is he unsophisticated or naïve.

Descartes's procedure in conducting his inquiry within this unsophisticated framework is not arbitrary. In the First Meditation, after all, the position of common sense can be criticized only by using its own resources, for Descartes has as yet no other resources to bring to bear against it. He has no vantage point external to the common-sense position he is examining, since he has emptied his mind, and he can make use only of materials provided by that position itself. The only question he can ask about common sense is whether it enables solutions to be given to the problems that it itself recognizes as needing to be solved.

When Descartes affirms that dreams occur, accordingly, he is not betraying his resolution to suspend all judgments. The occurrence of dreams is an element in the common-sense picture of experience. In the statement that he is "a man who is used to sleeping at night and experiencing in dreams . . . ," Descartes goes no further than he went in his earlier assertion that knowledge comes to him from or through the senses. Sensory experience includes dreaming, and the belief that dreams occur is on a par with the belief that waking sense perception occurs. Both beliefs belong to the position that he is examining in order to bring out its inadequacy. In effect, then, Descartes is asking himself this: Supposing that sense perception (including dreams) occurs, is it possible to find certainty in it? He adopts the position of common sense as a working hypothesis in order to test its viability. His procedure does not require him to accept its doctrines in any sense more substantial than this.

It is important to understand why Descartes does not treat dreaming simply as a special case of perceiving under non-ideal conditions. When an object is distant or the light is poor, the fact that these unfavorable conditions prevail can be observed and taken into account even by someone who is limited to sensory experience. The senses themselves provide the basis, in such cases, for deciding whether or not their testimony is to be accepted. On the other hand, "one can never by any certain indications distinguish being awake from dreaming." A dreamer can find no reliable sensory indication that the conditions of his perceiving are not ideal.

The import of the dream argument is that even if Descartes makes the most generous assumptions and supposes that he is a normal perceiver who obtains sensory data under conditions favorable in every respect *discoverable by the senses*, he cannot be certain that the sensory data he obtains will be veridical. Even when it is attempted under the most suitable conditions *that the senses can select*, discrimination between veridical and non-veridical data *with the senses alone* remains uncertain. Descartes's third version of the principle concerning sensory evidence is therefore unacceptable. Even on their own best terms, the senses are incapable of providing certainty. Following the policy of relying exclusively upon the senses for knowledge of the physical world leads to an impasse. The policy defeats itself, in a sense, for it requires making distinctions that cannot be made within the limits it prescribes.

5

THE STRATEGY
OF THE FIRST MEDITATION

Descartes's critique of the senses does not end with the collapse of his third attempt to formulate a reliable principle of sensory evidence. Common sense has still further resources, beyond those his inquiry has already exhausted, and he calls upon them immediately after he presents the dream argument. In doing so he shifts the focus of his investigation. Since his attempt to arrive at a reliable procedure for finding certainty about the existence of physical objects has failed, he turns to a search for certainty about the elements of which these objects are in some sense composed. This leads him to discuss "simpler and more universal things" and mathematics, and finally to develop his famous argument concerning the possibility that a malign deity or demon condemns him inescapably to being deceived. I wish to postpone examining these sequels to the dream argument, however, in order to make some additional comments on the portion of Descartes's critique of the senses already discussed.

The distinction between real and illusory sensory objects, or between veridical and non-veridical perception, plays a fundamental role in Descartes's examination of sensory evidence. Yet he makes no effort in the First Meditation to explicate the distinction; he offers no account of the contrasts he invokes between physical objects or events and dream imagery, or between the real and the illusory in perception. It would be a mistake, however, to reproach him for failing to do so. Far from undermining the rigor and value of his argument, the omission of such an explication is in fact essential to the point Descartes wishes the First Meditation to make. For what he is anxious to show is precisely that the distinction between acceptable and unacceptable beliefs cannot be construed adequately in sensory terms. His examination of sensory evidence may be understood as a series of attempts to arrive at a viable formulation of the distinction between veridical and non-veridical perception. And his point is that while those who rely entirely on the senses need to make use of this distinction, they cannot make the distinction good because it cannot be drawn in sensory terms alone.

But how can Descartes show that the senses are deceptive if he does not have the criterion for distinguishing between the real and the illusory with which an analysis of this distinction would provide him? This question arises with the very first sentence of his examination of the senses, in which he says that he has "caught them deceiving." Descartes gives no account of how he managed to catch the senses in their deception. It is possible to construct a reasonable account of the matter, however, which illuminates the entire structure of his inquiry in the First Meditation.

There is an important difference between finding on the one hand that the senses are deceptive and, on the other, that a given sensory object is illusory or that a given perception is non-veridical. It is possible to accomplish the latter only with the help of a criterion for illusion or perceptual error, but to accomplish the former such a criterion is not necessary. To find that the senses are deceptive involves discovering that some sensory objects are illusory, but it does not necessarily involve identifying the illusory ones. What is essential is simply to find that not all of a given set of sensory objects can be real, and this becomes clear whenever one sensory experience conflicts with another. When Descartes remarks that the deceptiveness of the senses has been proven to him, he has in mind nothing more than commonplace conflicts of experience, for example, those that occur when a given object is first observed from a distance and then examined from nearby.

A line may appear straight from a distance and curved from nearby. Insofar as judgments are based directly and simply on the senses, conflicting testimony of this sort leads to incompatible judgments—that the line is straight and that it is curved. It is possible to escape uncertainty concerning which judgment to accept only if there is a way of deciding which testimony takes precedence and which is to be discounted. Otherwise, there is as much reason to accept the one judgment as the other. Even if the testimony concerning a given matter is consistent, moreover, no judgment based on it can be accepted as unshakably certain unless there is a satisfactory procedure for resolving conflicts. For the recognition that conflicting testimony may eventually come along will make it impossible to regard any judgment as enjoying the permanence Descartes demands of scientific beliefs.

Since it leads to inconsistent results, the policy of indiscriminately accepting all sensory testimony at its face value is a poor one for somebody who is seeking certainty. The problem Descartes faces is to formulate an alternative policy in terms of which no judgment will be certified except those that cannot be shaken by conflicting testimony. His initial approach to this problem is to try to identify a class of perceptions with greater authority than any others—a class of privileged perceptions that may be given precedence over any other perceptions whose testimony conflicts with theirs. In making this attempt, Descartes is doing just what the terms of his inquiry demand: he is following the lead of common sense, which accords a final authority to the perceptions of normal observers under ideal conditions.

But is the testimony of these perceptions unequivocal, so that the policy of accepting it will lead only to unshakable judgments; or is there reason to fear conflict even among the most privileged perceptions themselves? Common sense ordinarily takes for granted that judgments based on such perceptions are mutually consistent. When a conflict between perceptions occurs, the natural response of common sense is to assume that at least one of the perceivers is defective or that at least one of the conflicting perceptions occurred under imperfect external conditions.

Even within the ordinary purview of common sense, however, the policy of relying on privileged perceptions encounters a difficulty in connection with the occurrence of dreams. What a person dreams often conflicts with what he perceives when awake; thus judgments based on dream experience may subsequently be contradicted by judgments based on waking perceptions, and vice versa. If it were possible to distinguish between the imagery of dreams on the one hand and waking perceptions on the other, these contradictions would be no more serious than the contradictions between privileged perceptions and less privileged ones. But Descartes maintains that the distinction cannot satisfactorily be made within the framework his inquiry provides.

In order to identify members of the class of privileged perceptions it is necessary to evaluate the conditions under which perceptions take place. Now this can be done only on the basis of sensory testimony. A preference for perceptions of nearby objects over perceptions of objects at a great distance, for example, can be implemented only by relying on sensory estimates of distance; similarly, it is only by the use of the senses that a person can determine whether the light in which some visual observation occurs is bright or dim. Privileged perceptions can be distinguished from others, then, only by various sensory marks. Now the point of the dream argument is that any sensory mark may characterize dream perceptions as well as waking ones. Hume evidently thought that sensory data produced by the mind itself could be distinguished from "original sentiments" by their lesser "force and vivacity." Descartes briefly considers the similar notion that "a sleeping man would not have such distinct experiences." He quickly realizes, however, that dream images need not be "faint and dull," as Hume would have it, but may have as much force and vivacity as any sensory data.

Since he "can never by any certain indications distinguish being awake from dreaming," Descartes concludes, a dreamer has no grounds for discounting the weight of his experience if he dreams that ideal conditions for perception prevail. Whatever sensory criteria a person relies upon for identifying privileged perceptions, therefore, they fail to discriminate conclusively between such perceptions and at least some dream perceptions. Hence if someone's policy is to accept the testimony of whatever bears the sensory marks of privileged perceptions, he may be led to accept the testimony of some dream perceptions. Descartes regards this as sufficient to discredit his third version of the sensory principle.

Within the framework of common sense as he has developed it so far, Descartes is unable to attain his goal of certainty concerning what exists. Because the senses provide conflicting testimony, he attempts to classify perceptions into those that reveal existence and those that do not. But the resources the senses make available are inadequate to enable him to accomplish this classification. In the dream argument he recognizes that conflicts may occur among perceptions of *any* sort—even among those that bear the sensory marks of perception under the most ideal conditions. Since he can identify no reliable sensory differentia of dreams and waking perceptions under ideal conditions, he is forced to acknowledge that even the third version of his common-sense principle may lead him to accept mutually inconsistent judgments.

As he considers each of the various versions of this principle, Descartes may be understood to ask the following question: Given that a judgment has been made in accordance with this version of the principle, is there any reasonable ground for doubting it? He does not explain what is to count as a reasonable ground for doubt, but it is possible to construct an explanation on the basis of the way in which he actually conducts his critique of the senses. In rejecting each of the three versions of the principle that he examines, he offers an alternative interpretation of the evidence with which the principle is concerned. That is, he shows that the evidence the principle presumes to be sufficient for establishing the existence of something is in fact consistent with its non-existence.

Thus sensory data presented under unknown conditions may consistently be regarded as having arisen out of conditions unfavorable for perceiving and therefore as not revealing the existence and character of a real object; testimony obtained indiscriminately, in accordance with the first version of the principle, is therefore open to conflicting interpretations. The second version of the principle limits the sensory testimony on which judgments may be based to that obtained under ideal external conditions; but the weight of this testimony can consistently be denied by ascribing the data to imperfections in the observer. The third version of the principle eliminates this difficulty by insisting upon evidence obtained by a normal perceiver under ideal conditions; but this version of the principle fails too, since perceptions that seem to fulfill its demands may be indistinguishable from those in dreams. Hence conflicting interpretations seem to be available even with regard to sensory testimony that is apparently of the most privileged sort.

The recognition of a possibility is sufficient to provide a reasonable ground for doubt. Now it is worth noticing that a ground for doubt may be reasonable in one set of circumstances but unreasonable in others. If a person knows nothing about the conditions under which some perception has occurred, for example, he must acknowledge the possibility that the conditions were unfavorable for accurate perception. But if he confines his attention to sensory data that he knows have been obtained under ideal conditions, it is not reasonable for him to entertain the possibility that these data are misleading because of unfavorable conditions. Moreover, concepts or statements that seem at one time to be quite coherent may turn out to involve logical inconsistencies that were previously unsuspected.

Near the end of the First Meditation, for example, Descartes advances as a reasonable ground for doubting various matters the possibility that there is an omnipotent demon who devotes his energies to deception. Now the existence of such a being is logically impossible, according to the position he develops later in the *Meditations*, because a malicious nature is a sign of weakness and is therefore not compatible with omnipotence: "although the ability to deceive may seem to be evidence of cunning or of power, there is no doubt that an intent to deceive testifies to malice or weakness and therefore does not characterize God."[1] But Descartes does not recognize, in the First Meditation, that the notion of a being both omnipotent and evil is logically incoherent. And as long as the existence of the demon *seems* possible to him, it provides him with what he must take to be a reasonable ground for doubt.

Late in the First Meditation, Descartes says that "of those things I formerly considered to be true there is nothing regarding which it is not legitimate to doubt . . . not through lack of consideration or frivolity, but for valid and meditated reasons." The things to which the phrase "those things I formerly considered to be true" refers should not be understood to include logical truths; the phrase refers only to sensory beliefs, since it is these alone that Descartes is aware of holding. Even with regard to these beliefs, however, it is only from the common-sense point of view adopted in the First Meditation that his reasons for doubt impress Descartes as valid and well thought through. What seems reasonable to him in this context may not, and in fact does not, also seem reasonable to him from the more sophisticated and mature point of view he develops in later Meditations.

In his synopsis of the *Meditations*, Descartes qualifies his endorsement of the grounds for doubt set forth in the First Meditation "about all things and especially about material things." These doubts are reasonable, he observes, "as long as we do not have other foundations for the sciences than those we have had before now."[2] It would be a mistake to suppose that Descartes regards his critique of the senses in the First Meditation as establishing that no sensory beliefs can be certain. The critique is designed to show, at the most, that no such beliefs can reasonably be regarded as certain by someone who has no resources other than those provided by common sense. But even if the senses cannot themselves provide a foundation for the sciences, it is another question entirely whether cer-

---

[1] Fourth Meditation, HR I, 172; AT VII, 53, ll. 25-29. In the *Conversation with Burman* Descartes refers to his hypothesis of an omnipotent deceiver in the First Meditation and says that the hypothesis is self-contradictory. See AT V, 146, 150-151.

[2] HR I, 140; AT VII, 12, ll. 3-4.

tainty in sensory matters can reasonably be attained once a sound philosophical foundation for knowledge has been constructed.

In the course of the First Meditation Descartes considers two general strategies for finding certainty. The first involves trying to identify a class of sensory experiences that are more reliable than any others and that may reasonably be accepted with unreserved confidence. He abandons this strategy when the dream argument shows him that no identification of such a class can be accomplished by the senses. But even if it could, Descartes would still have had to face a serious problem. He might reasonably regard any member of the privileged class as immune to criticism based on experience outside the class, but the possibility would remain that one member of the class might be criticized on the basis of another equally privileged member of the class. In other words, Descartes would have had to face the question of whether it is reasonable to be confident that judgments based on privileged experiences are mutually consistent. In a later chapter I shall attempt to show that this is precisely the sort of question he does face when he considers the reliability of clear and distinct perceptions. The substance of his "metaphysical doubt" concerning clear and distinct perception, I shall maintain, is the fear that judgments based on clear and distinct perceptions may be mutually inconsistent.

The First Meditation's second strategy, to which Descartes turns after the dream argument, ignores the question of which sensory experiences are the most reliable. It consists of an attempt to identify something that can be learned from *any* sensory experience at all. Subsequent chapters below will consider how Descartes pursues this strategy through his discussions of imagination and of the simples, until his inability to account for the origin of human faculties shows him that the assumptions on which the strategy is based are questionable. Both his first and his second strategies fail because the common-sense framework within which he is working in the First Meditation cannot provide a satisfactory answer to a question upon which confidence in the strategy depends. In the case of the first strategy it is a question about whether sensory experience is part of a dream; in the case of the second, about the inherent nature of the mind.

It may clarify the character of Descartes's inquiry, and focus the light shed by the First Meditation on the nature of his enterprise, if my earlier remarks on the dream argument are extended. I shall make the points I have in mind by discussing certain rather typical misconceptions, which are exhibited in a recent book by W. H. Walsh.[3] Walsh misconstrues both the logical character of the argument as it appears in the First Meditation and its substance. He begins by characterizing the argument as one in which "the initial premise is that we sometimes take objects to exist in reality when they exist only in our dreams and the conclusion [is] that we may be dreaming all the time." He then goes on to say that Descartes's reasoning suffers from "a fundamental incoherence . . . springing from the fact that if the conclusion is true the premises cannot be set up." His point is this:

> Suppose that it were indeed the case that not one of our perceptual experiences could be warranted as reliable: we should never be in a position to say that we are sometimes deceived in our sense-judgments, for in the circumstances envisaged we should not know what it was not to be so deceived. In order to decide that we were mistaken on a particular occasion we need to be able to contrast the experience we had then with others which we take to be non-deceptive; if no sense-experience can be taken as being in order the contrast cannot be made. Similarly with dreaming. Were it really the case that, as Descartes puts it, 'there exist no certain marks' by which to distinguish waking from dreaming, we could never formulate the premise that we sometimes think we are perceiving things when all the time we are dreaming. It would not be possible to say, as Descartes wants to say, things like 'I thought I was awake and sitting in my room, but it subsequently turned out that I was dreaming.'

According to Walsh, then, the conclusion of the dream argument entails that it is impossible to distinguish between deceptive and non-deceptive experience. But the premises of the argument, as he understands them, involve the use of this distinction. This is why he claims that if the conclusion of the argument is true its premises cannot meaningfully be asserted, and that the argument exhibits "a fundamental incoherence."

Walsh clearly wishes to maintain not only that the dream argument's conclusion is incoherent with its premises but also that this suffices to discredit the argument. Even granting the incoherence, however, it does not follow that the argument fails. Walsh does not indicate whether he thinks the argument's conclusion is derived validly from its premises. But if it is, and if Walsh is correct

[3] W. H. Walsh, *Metaphysics* (London: Hutchinson University Library, 1963), p. 91. All quotations from Walsh are from this page of his book.

in claiming that the conclusion entails that its premises cannot properly be asserted, then the incoherence of the conclusion with the premises discredits not the argument but the premises. Far from being a defect in the argument, this would mean that the argument is a successful one of the *reductio* type. It serves to undermine its premises by showing that they entail their own unacceptability.

Now it is in fact Descartes's intention to show that the common-sense position in terms of which the dream argument is formulated turns upon itself in a self-destructive way. The development of a *reductio* argument is accordingly a most appropriate procedure for him to follow. Indeed he could hardly hope to proceed in any other way, for in criticizing the position that the senses can provide knowledge he has no legitimate alternative but to develop an argument internal to that position. His resolution to suspend all judgments deprives him of the right to bring to bear against common sense any principles other than its own. His demonstration of the inadequacy of common sense must rely entirely upon materials that common sense provides, since he is entitled to use no others. The *reductio* style of argument is not only appropriate to his purposes, therefore, but uniquely suited to them.

Thus Walsh misses the point of Descartes's reasoning. Moreover, he misconstrues the substance of the dream argument as well as its intent. Descartes's conclusion is not, as Walsh supposes, that "we may be dreaming all the time." His point about dreams is simply that "I can never by any certain indications distinguish being awake from dreaming." Walsh may think that this commits Descartes to the further claim that we may be dreaming all the time. It is not at all evident that this is so, however, and in any case Descartes draws no such conclusion in his discussion of the matter in the First Meditation. He is interested only in bringing out the impossibility of discriminating with certainty, on the basis of sensory data alone, between dream experience and experience of the real world. Perhaps it is fair to regard him as committed to the view that, so far as what the senses reveal goes, we may be dreaming at *any* time. But this is not the same as the assertion that we may be dreaming at *all* times.

Nothing in the text of the *Meditations* supports Walsh's formulation of the conclusion of the dream argument. On the other hand, there are at least two strong indications in the text that the dream argument is not supposed to raise the possibility that we may always be dreaming. First, the theory of imagination that Descartes formulates immediately after the dream argument presupposes that we have some veridical experience which provides us with materials out of which the fantasies of dreams can be constructed. Second, if the dream argument did conclude that all perceptions may be non-veridical, Descartes could hope to rebut it only by showing either that it is not possible that we should always be dreaming or that we do not in fact always dream. When he comes to rebutting the dream argument in the Sixth Meditation, however, this is not what he attempts to do. His rebuttal consists merely in an explanation of how it is after all possible to discriminate with certainty between dream experience and experience of the real world. This suggests strongly that the dream argument is to be understood as undermining confidence in our ability to discriminate between veridical and non-veridical perception, and not as raising the possibility that all perception is non-veridical.

The same point also comes out clearly in *Principles of Philosophy* where, after calling attention to the occurrence of dreams, Descartes says: "no signs appear by which [a man] may with certainty distinguish being asleep from being awake."[4] Here again the point is not that we may always be dreaming but that we cannot tell when we are dreaming. Walsh's interpretation is not without some basis, however, for in both the *Discourse on Method* and *The Search After Truth* Descartes himself appears to formulate the conclusion Walsh ascribes to him. In the *Discourse* he says: "Since all the same thoughts that we have while awake may also come to us while we sleep, without any of them being at that time true, I resolved to suppose that everything that had ever entered my mind was no more true than the illusions of my dreams."[5] And in *The Search After Truth*, the observation that men dream is followed by this question: "How can you be certain that your life is not a continual dream and that everything you believe you learn by means of your senses is not as false as it is when you are asleep?"[6] From a consideration of all these texts, one might easily be led to infer that Descartes himself was not altogether clear about precisely what conclusion he thought the dream argument justified.

Three points, however, need to be made. First, the *Discourse* and *The Search After Truth* may reasonably be regarded as less au-

---

[4] *Principles of Philosophy*, Part I, Principle 4; AT VIII, 6, ll. 5-7.
[5] *Discourse on Method*, HR I, 101; AT VI, 32, ll. 9-15.
[6] *The Search After Truth*, HR I, 314; AT X, 511, ll. 22-25.

thoritative on technical matters than the *Meditations* or the *Principles*. The former works were written in French for a more popular audience than the latter, and Descartes did not publish *The Search After Truth* at all. Second, there is no ambiguity in Descartes's treatment of dreaming in the *Meditations* or in the *Principles*. Finally, neither in the *Discourse* nor in *The Search After Truth* is the argument about the demon distinguished from the dream argument. This suggests that the dream argument came to have a weaker conclusion in the later works than it had in the earlier ones because Descartes took away part of the function he had assigned to the dream argument in the earlier works and assigned it in his more systematic treatises to the argument about the demon.

6

SIMPLE AND
UNIVERSAL THINGS

The dream argument purports to show that a person who is committed to relying for knowledge upon the senses alone cannot distinguish, among the things of which he is aware, between physical objects or events and dream images. If he insists upon remaining firm in his commitment to the senses, therefore, he can hope to acquire only such knowledge as does not depend upon making this distinction. Now since Descartes is playing the role of someone who has made this commitment, his problem after the dream argument is to determine whether knowledge can be based on sensory experience in a way that avoids the necessity for distinguishing between veridical and non-veridical data. Accordingly he attempts to formulate a version of his principle that will lead him from sensory data to knowledge whether the data are veridical or not. He first considers a version based on a certain theory about the imagination, but is soon led, when it develops that this theory needs revision, to a more sophisticated formulation.

According to the theory Descartes invokes immediately subsequent to the dream argument, the imagination models dream images after objects or events that are not themselves imaginary. As he explains the matter, "it surely must be acknowledged that things seen during sleep are like painted representations, which could not be formed except in the likeness of truly real things." Even if it is only the illusion of a dream that we "open our eyes, move our head, extend our hands," nevertheless we can affirm confidently that "things of these kinds—eyes, head, hands, and the whole body—exist as real things, not imaginary, but true." Descartes's idea seems to be that while the particular objects or events in our dreams may not be real, there must be real objects or events of the same general sorts as those in our dreams or at least of the same general sorts as the parts of those dream objects and events. There need be no real body identical with or even exactly like the body of which a man dreams, but there must be real bodies; or at any rate there must be real things like the dreamed body's parts. In other words, the reproductions of which dreams consist can differ from their real counterparts only in detail or in the arrangement of their parts.

This account construes dreams as analogous to paintings, with imagination playing the role of the painter. And "even when painters themselves strive to depict sirens and satyrs with the most extraordinary forms, they cannot provide them with natures that are novel in every respect, but can only mix together the parts of different animals." In terms of this rather naïvely commonsensical empiricist theory a dreamer must have had some experience of the real world; otherwise his imagination would not have the necessary models after which to fashion a dream. In any case, the version of the principle that is implicit in Descartes's account is something like this: It is reasonable to accept beliefs concerning the existence of things that correspond to the parts of sensory objects or events, but it is not safe to believe in the existence of objects that correspond to the complex wholes of these objects or events.

This "solution" to the problem of arriving at certainty is clearly defective. It is too vague to provide adequate instructions for identifying either the elements of which a dream object is composed or the general kinds of things of which the elements are counterparts. But while Descartes is quick to alter his account, it is not this defect that he seeks to repair. What strikes him as requiring correction is the assumption that the imagination is helpless to fashion images without a model. This limitation seems to him inaccurate and arbitrary, and he immediately concedes that a person may after all imagine novelties that are unlike real things even in a general way.

The work of imagination does not, then, depend upon models. But still, Descartes reflects, it surely requires materials; and these, it seems, can come only from reality. Painters may "think up something so novel that nothing at all like it had been seen." But while their work may represent something "entirely fictitious and false, at least the colors out of which they compose it would surely have to be true colors." And by the same token, "even if things of these kinds—eyes, head, hands, and the like—could be imaginary, still it must be acknowledged that certain other simpler and more universal things are true and that out of these 'true colors' are formed all the true and the false representations of real things in our thought." Descartes revises the principle, then, so that it recommends accepting beliefs in the reality of the simple and universal elements of which he says sensory objects are formed: for instance, "corporeal nature in general and its extension, the shape of extended things, the quantity (or the size and number) of those things, the place in which they exist, the time through which they last, and the like." The imagination merely arranges elements that are given to it. Like a nonfigurative painter, it may free itself entirely from dependence on models. But its freedom is limited, for it has no power to originate the elementary materials with which it works. Imaginary things are necessarily composites; the simple cannot be fictitious but must be real.

Several questions are raised by this version of the sensory principle and by the theory of imagination upon which it depends. What are the criteria of simplicity and universality? How are simplicity and universality related: are the simples of which Descartes speaks necessarily universal, or *vice versa*, or what? Are all simples and universals characteristic of every sensory object or may a sensory object be characterized by only some of them? These are obvious questions, which have to be answered before the principle can be fully intelligible. Descartes, however, does not even consider them.

Martial Gueroult interprets the simple and universal things as necessary conditions of the possibility of any sensory presentation; nothing can be sensed, he maintains, unless it exhibits them.[1] If this interpretation is correct, an argument is readily available to show that whatever is universal must also be simple. For if the universals must characterize *all* sensory data, then the imagination cannot fabricate them out of elements found in certain sensory data, since the universals must also characterize these data. Hence if they are necessary conditions for any sensory presentation, universals cannot be fabricated out of sensory materials at all and must, at least in this sense, be simple. As for the alternative of fabricating them somehow out of non-sensory materials, even if this is intelligible no such materials can be considered by Descartes at a stage of the *Meditations* where he is still supposing that all knowledge is sensory. In any case, however, Gueroult offers no evidence for his interpretation, and neither he nor Descartes presents the argument I have just formulated concerning the simplicity of the universal.

The passage in the First Meditation that I am currently considering seems to involve a defect even more egregious than Descartes's failure to elucidate his theory of the imagination and the version of

[1] Martial Gueroult, *Descartes selon l'ordre des raisons* (Paris: Aubier, 1953), Vol. I, p. 36.

56

his principle based upon it. For what right has he to present *any* theory of the imagination at all, at a point in his investigations where he presumably knows nothing and is still bound by his resolve to empty his mind of all opinions? How can he be entitled to remark, for instance, that "it surely must be acknowledged that things seen during sleep are like painted representations, which could not be formed except in the likeness of truly real things"? Is it legitimate for Descartes, who is supposed to have suspended all judgments without exception, to assert that "painters . . . only mix together the parts of different animals," and that even if a painting is not a copy of reality, "at least the colors . . . would surely have to be true colors"? Whence these alleged facts and certainties, which Descartes has surely not established in the course of his inquiry? What justifies his speaking of the origin of dreams, or of the nature and limits of the imagination?

If Descartes actually assumed the truth of these assertions and really propounded these theories, he would blatantly violate the conditions he sets for the conduct of his inquiry in the *Meditations.* He does not in fact assume their truth, however, and nothing in his discussion requires him to do so. This does not mean that he regards the assertions and theories in question as false. Indeed most commentators agree that the theory of simple and universal things sketched in the First Meditation is an important doctrine of his philosophy. I do wish to insist, nevertheless, that he does not present this theory in the First Meditation as a doctrine to which he is committed or upon the truth of which the argument of the *Meditations* essentially depends.

Whose doctrine is it, then, and what argument does depend upon it? The answer is clear: It is a doctrine advanced in behalf of common sense. Descartes does not assume that he knows what stuff dreams are made on. He is not developing his own position in the passage at all; rather, he is exploring the resources of common sense. It is not Descartes himself but his hypothetical believer in the sufficiency of the senses who turns, after the dream argument, to an account of imagination that connects dreams to reality, and who relies so naïvely on the superficially plausible analogy between painting and imagining.

To be sure, it is Descartes who presents the views of common sense and he attempts to develop them as cogently as their inherent limitations permit. The crude theory of the imagination with which he starts is one that might naturally occur to a man in the street, but Descartes quickly replaces it with a more sophisticated version.

Not only is the man in the street likely to refine his opinions once he makes them explicit; it is also important for Descartes's purpose to consider the strongest position that can be developed within the context defined by the dogma that all knowledge is attained by means of the senses. He would not accomplish much, after all, by revealing the inadequacy of an unnecessarily weak version of common sense. In order for his critique to be significant and conclusive, it must confront the best that common sense can provide. Descartes's purpose also explains why he does not fully develop the views he presents. For he introduces them only in order to reveal their inadequacy, and the argument by which he ultimately accomplishes this does not depend upon the details of their explication. Thus it is sufficient for him to sketch the theories in question in a more or less general way.

Even some of Descartes's best critics have misunderstood the status of the views presented during his critique of the senses. Gueroult mistakenly takes the First Meditation as an authentic account of Descartes's own philosophical doctrines, and cites it in order to establish that Descartes holds the theories of imagination and of simple and universal things presented there.[2] Jean Laporte makes a similar error when he asserts that "la Première Méditation notait que toutes nos idées sont formées, quant à leurs éléments, à la ressemblance de certaines représentations génériques."[3]

Now it may well be that Descartes does accept the doctrines in question; his acceptance of *some such* doctrines can hardly be disputed. But that he accepts them cannot be inferred from the fact that he presents them in the First Meditation. It can be established only by evidence from elsewhere in his works, where he is writing to express his own views and not just to characterize positions without committing himself to them. This is not a trivial restriction. In the discussion of simples in the First Meditation, for example, there are references to color which suggest that it is among the things spoken of there as irreducible and necessarily real. Gueroult improperly and futilely cites these references as his *only* support for the important claim that Descartes regards sensory qualities as among the simple and universal things.[4]

The account of simple and universal things given in the First

---

[2] *Descartes selon l'ordre des raisons*, pp. 34-35.
[3] Jean Laporte, *Le rationalisme de Descartes* (Paris: Presses Universitaires de France, 1950), p. 103, note 7.
[4] *Descartes selon l'ordre des raisons*, pp. 34-35.

Meditation does, as a matter of fact, differ significantly from Descartes's own theory. Since my approach to the *Meditations* is consecutive rather than topical, it would be out of place to examine these differences here in detail. I will, however, briefly consider two closely related points in which the First Meditation quite unmistakably fails to express Descartes's views properly.

First, the account of simples in the First Meditation does not include Descartes's characteristic claim that our ideas of these things are innate. On the contrary, indeed, it takes for granted that a person's possession of these ideas derives from his prior acquaintance with the simples in reality. Second, the list of simples that Descartes gives in the First Meditation includes examples from only two of the four classes of simples that he himself distinguished. It includes some (e.g., quantity) that pertain to whatever is conceivable, and some (e.g., figure) that pertain to bodies in particular. None of his examples, however, pertains particularly either to the mind, or to the body and the mind taken together. On the other hand, Descartes gives the following account of his own theory, which involves a fourfold division of simples, in a letter to Princess Elisabeth dated 21 May 1643:

> *I believe we have in us certain primitive notions that are, so to speak, the originals on the pattern of which we form all our other knowledge. There are only a few such notions. For besides the most general of them—being, number, duration, etc.—which pertain to everything we can conceive, we have only, for body in particular, the notion of extension, from which those of figure and of movement follow; and for the soul itself, we have only that of thought, in which the perceptions of the intellect and the inclinations of the will are included. Finally, for the soul and the body taken together we have only the notion of their union, upon which depends the notion of the force that the soul has to move the body and that the body has to act upon the soul in causing its feelings and its passions.*[5]

It is easy to explain, of course, why the First Meditation provides no examples either of simples pertaining to the mind alone or of simples pertaining to the body and the mind taken together. In the First Meditation, where Descartes is supposing that all knowledge is sensory, there is room in his account for what pertains to physical or sensory things and, of course, for what pertains indifferently to everything. But there is no room for what pertains only to non-

---

[5]   AT III, 664-665.

sensory things, e.g., to the mind. The mind does not come to the attention of Descartes's inquiry until the Second Meditation, when his examination of sensory beliefs has been completed. Moreover, the fact that he presumes in the First that the senses alone are the source of all knowledge also explains why he does not there propound his doctrine that simple ideas are innate.

7 MATHEMATICS IN THE FIRST MEDITATION

My claim that the First Meditation deals only with material provided by the senses appears to conflict with the fact that it includes a discussion of mathematical propositions. Surely the senses do not determine that a square has four sides or that two and three make five. These seem to be paradigms of what, according to Descartes, we perceive clearly and distinctly through the understanding or reason. In his view reason, not sense perception, enables us to know such truths. Why, then, does he consider mathematical propositions in a context that is presumably limited to sensory beliefs?

The answer lies in the fact, to which I have already given so much emphasis, that the doctrines Descartes presents or assumes in the First Meditation are not necessarily his own. He conducts his discussion of mathematical propositions from the point of view of the naïve empiricism whose inadequacies he is seeking to expose, and this discussion does not reflect his own more sophisticated conception of mathematics. Despite appearances to the contrary, therefore, it is a mistake to suppose that the First Meditation deals first with sensory beliefs and then, after the dream argument, with beliefs of reason. The rational faculty, as something distinct from the senses, does not come to the explicit attention of Descartes's inquiry until considerably later in the *Meditations*.

It is somewhat imprecise to say, as I have just now and at other times said, that the First Meditation considers only material provided by the senses. It is more accurate to say that the First Meditation considers only material that the naïve empiricist, in behalf of whom its argument is conducted, *thinks* the senses provide. Now it is characteristic of such a person, as it is of those geometers who cannot free themselves of dependence on a drawn figure, that he is incapable of considering anything in decisive and unequivocal ab-

straction from a sensory context. He ascribes to the senses, therefore, many things that are not properly to be found in them.

Descartes makes this clear in the *Conversation with Burman*. In
a passage already cited he deals with an objection to his statement
that he has learned from or through the senses everything he has
"accepted until now as true in the highest degree." Burman had
evidently argued during the conversation that Descartes was mistaken in this, and had pointed out that not only various abstract
principles and necessary truths but also the ideas of ourselves and
of God cannot be accounted for by reference to the senses alone.
As Descartes explains, however, this objection misses the point. It
fails to recognize the fictitious identity assumed in the First Meditation:

> One cannot object here that general principles and ideas of God
> and of ourselves, which have never been in the senses, have been
> omitted. For, in the first place, even they are acquired through the
> senses—that is, through hearing. In the second place, the author
> is considering here a man who is first beginning to philosophize
> and who attends only to those things with which he knows him-
> self to be acquainted. For as regards general principles and axi-
> oms—for example, it is impossible that the same thing should be
> and should not be—men limited to the senses, as we all are before
> [we encounter] philosophy, do not consider or attend to them. But
> since [these principles and axioms] are, clearly, innate and ex-
> perienced inwardly, [such men] neglect them; they do not con-
> sider them except in a confused way—never in the abstract and
> separated from matter and from particular instances. For if men
> did consider them in the latter way, no one would have any
> doubts about them. And if the skeptics had done so, no one would
> ever have been a skeptic, since those [principles and axioms]
> cannot be denied by anyone who regards them attentively.[1]

What Descartes says here about "general principles and axioms"
applies equally to the propositions of mathematics and to such ideas
as those of God and of the mind. If the philosophical novices whose
unsophisticated empiricism is at issue in the First Meditation are
aware of these propositions and ideas at all, they are aware of them
only "confusedly and never in the abstract, separated from matter
and from particular instances." They do not examine them "attentively." In other words they do not perceive them clearly and

[1] AT V, 146; Charles Adam, ed., *Entretien avec Burman* (Paris: Boivin, 1937),
pp. 3-5. My emphasis.

distinctly. If they did so, they would find it impossible to doubt them.

It is essential to understand that when Descartes discusses mathematical propositions in the First Meditation, he regards them as *not* being perceived clearly and distinctly. They are being considered there by someone "who is first beginning to philosophize"—someone who is still bound to the senses, "as we all are before [we encounter] philosophy." It is this person, whose identity Descartes assumes, who conducts the First Meditation's critique of the senses; and this person's apprehension of the objects of reason is invariably mixed up with sense perception. He learns to use his reason independently and attentively only at a later stage in the progress of his inquiry.

Descartes maintains that it is impossible to doubt what is being clearly and distinctly perceived. He enunciates this doctrine in a number of places, among them the final section of the passage just quoted from the *Conversation with Burman*. There he observes that when general principles or axioms are being considered "attentively," rather than "confusedly," it is impossible to doubt them. Since skeptics do doubt them, skepticism must depend upon a failure to perceive them clearly and distinctly. It can be inferred, by the same token, that whoever is considering the mathematical propositions discussed in the First Meditation cannot be perceiving them clearly and distinctly. For since he proceeds to doubt them, he must be considering them in the confused manner that the *Conversation with Burman* describes as characteristic of those at a primitive level of philosophical development.

Haldane and Ross make it unnecessarily difficult for those who rely on their translation of the First Meditation to understand this point. According to their text, Descartes says of the mathematical propositions he considers that "it does not seem possible that truths so clear and apparent can be suspected of any falsity." The phrase "clear and apparent" tends to suggest the phrase "clear and distinct," and this leads more or less naturally to the erroneous assumption that Descartes supposes the propositions in question to be clearly and distinctly perceived. But the phrase "clear and apparent" is not required either by the Latin original or by the French translation that Descartes himself approved. The Latin has *perspicuae veritates*, which may indeed be translated as "clear truths"; but Descartes generally uses the adjective *clarus* when he wishes to speak of the clarity of clear and distinct perception. The contemporary French translator quite sensibly uses simply the adjective *apparent*, rather than *clair*, thereby muffling any allusion to clarity and distinctness. Haldane and Ross, on the other hand, evidently unwilling or unable to construe Descartes's intention, attempt to play it safe by offering translations of *both* the Latin adjective *and* the French word that the authorized translation provides as its equivalent. In this way they unfortunately manage both to undo the good work of the French translator and, quite gratuitously, to select the most misleading equivalent available for the Latin term in question.

In any case, my interpretation does not need to rely for support either on an inference or on a disputed point concerning translation. For Descartes himself asserts quite explicitly that he supposes the mathematical propositions he discusses in the First Meditation to be perceived only confusedly. He makes this assertion in the course of considering a misunderstanding of the First Meditation on the part of the author of the Seventh Set of Objections. Of this critic Descartes remarks that

> *from the fact that I once said in Meditation One that there is nothing about which one may not be in doubt,* where I was supposing that I was not attending to anything that I perceived clearly, *he concludes that also in the following [Meditations] I can know nothing with certainty—as if the reasons we occasionally have for being in doubt about something were not legitimate and valid unless they proved that one must always be in doubt about that thing.*[2]

The emphasized clause hardly leaves any room for doubt that nothing discussed in the First Meditation is taken to be clearly and distinctly perceived.

It would not be necessary to review all this evidence were it not for the fact that the point I am making is often missed. According to Kemp Smith, for example, "Descartes is . . . insistent that all mathematical and other essences are . . . indubitable. They too, when experienced at all, are cognized in an immediate and therefore valid manner."[3] In support of this claim he quotes the following passage from the First Meditation:

> *For whether I am awake or asleep, two and three joined together are five, and a square does not have more than four sides. And*

[2] HR II, 266; AT VII, 460, ll. 21-29. My emphasis.
[3] Norman Kemp Smith, *New Studies in the Philosophy of Descartes* (London: Macmillan & Co., 1963), p. 272.

it seems that it cannot be the case that truths so evident should incur any suspicion of falsity.

Evidently Kemp Smith regards this passage as showing that Descartes thinks the mathematical propositions in question cannot be doubted. But the passage shows no such thing. It includes, to be sure, a remark by Descartes that it does not *seem* possible to doubt the propositions. But, in the first place, it is not Descartes but the inquirer of the First Meditation—a man committed to the senses and as yet uninitiated into the uses of reason—to whom it seems impossible to doubt them. Moreover, even this inquirer only at first thinks that doubt is impossible. He very quickly finds that he can doubt them after all.

Descartes does believe that what is being clearly and distinctly perceived cannot be doubted, and he does maintain that mathematical propositions of the types discussed in the First Meditation can be clearly and distinctly perceived. But Kemp Smith errs in the assumption he apparently makes that mathematical truths can be perceived only with clarity and distinctness and that they can therefore never be doubted at all. It is quite possible to think of true mathematical propositions without having clear and distinct perceptions of them, and the perception of them that figures in the First Meditation is in fact unclear.

There is very wide misunderstanding of Descartes's discussion of mathematical propositions in the First Meditation. Nearly all writers on the subject, in fact, seem to assume that Descartes is discussing propositions that are clearly and distinctly perceived. And this assumption naturally leads them to the mistaken conclusion that he introduces the *malin génie* in order to raise doubts that are somehow connected with clear and distinct perception.[4] This misunderstanding is quite serious. It not only reflects a general failure to grasp what is going on in the First Meditation, but has sometimes had a radical influence on wider interpretations of Descartes's metaphysical doubts and problems.

To illustrate how significant the misunderstanding may be, I shall briefly consider its effect on Kemp Smith's view of the metaphysical

---

[4] Cf. L. J. Beck, *The Method of Descartes* (Oxford: Clarendon Press, 1952), pp. 40, 272-273; Leonard Miller, "Descartes, Mathematics, and God," *Philosophical Review*, LXVI (1957), 451-452, 459; A. Boyce Gibson, *The Philosophy of Descartes* (London: Methuen & Co., 1932), pp. 307-309; Ferdinand Alquié, *Descartes, l'homme et l'oeuvre* (Paris: Presses Universitaires de France, 1956), p. 117; Henri Gouhier, *Essais sur Descartes* (Paris: J. Vrin, 1949), pp. 145-146; Martial Gueroult, *Descartes selon l'ordre des raisons* (Paris: Aubier, 1953), Vol. I, p. 36.

task Descartes faces in the *Meditations,* and then describe how another scholar, Willis Doney, is led by a rather different miscon-struction of the same matter to his particular interpretation of Descartes's enterprise. The point I wish to make just now is not that Kemp Smith and Doney misinterpret Descartes's metaphysical doubt, but rather that their interpretations—whether right or wrong —result from their misunderstandings of the role of mathematical propositions in the First Meditation.

Kemp Smith understands the doubts engendered by Descartes's notion that there may be an omnipotent and malicious demon as having to do with whether judgments such as those of mathematics "are or are not *eternally* true."[5] He believes that these doubts concern whether "what is true for us at one instant will hold true at other instants."[6] Now he seems to arrive at this interpretation of Descartes's metaphysical doubt in the following way. He starts by assuming that the mathematical propositions discussed in the First Meditation are being clearly and distinctly perceived. From this he concludes that it cannot be their truth that is doubted; for, as he points out, Descartes denies that it is possible to doubt anything that is being clearly and distinctly perceived. But the demon hypothesis obviously raises *some* sort of doubt about mathematical propositions. So Kemp Smith is led to suggest that the doubt con-cerns whether the truth of these propositions is "not merely for the moment but immutable."[7] His idea is apparently that an omnipo-tent demon might maliciously alter the truth-values of propositions so that what is known at one time to be true may at some other time be false. Descartes ultimately eliminates this possibility, according to Kemp Smith, with a "proof of the goodness and consequent immutability of God."[8]

Doney does not make the erroneous assumption from which Kemp Smith begins.[9] Indeed, he correctly infers from the fact that mathematical propositions are doubted in the First Meditation that Descartes is not perceiving them clearly and distinctly. But he misconstrues the alternative. Doney supposes that if Descartes asserts a mathematical proposition without having a clear and dis-tinct perception of it, then his assertion must be based on a proof

[5] Kemp Smith, *New Studies in the Philosophy of Descartes,* p. 272.
[6] *Ibid.,* p. 273.
[7] *Ibid.,* p. 274.
[8] *Ibid.,* p. 273.
[9] Willis Doney, "The Cartesian Circle," *Journal of the History of Ideas,* XVI (1955), esp. pp. 329-330.

consisting of a series of clear and distinct perceptions. Now to prove something requires, of course, a process of reasoning from one step to another, and in this process a step may be forgotten or remembered incorrectly. Doney explains the doubt of mathematical propositions in the First Meditation on the basis of the fact that the proofs by which he supposes these propositions to be known depend on memory. Mathematical propositions are subject to doubt because of the unreliability of memory, he maintains, and Descartes's interest in demonstrating God's existence is due to his need for a supernatural guarantee of the reliability of memory. Like Kemp Smith, Doney fails to recognize that in the First Meditation Descartes is apprehending the mathematical propositions in question only in a casual and confused manner and that there is consequently no particular difficulty in accounting for his ability to doubt them. Since there is no clear and distinct perception in the First Meditation, Doney and Kemp Smith are on the wrong track in their efforts to understand the doubts raised by the demon.

8

MATHEMATICS AND THE OMNIPOTENT DECEIVER

Since there are no clear and distinct perceptions in the First Meditation, it is obvious that Descartes does not introduce the demon in order to raise doubts about what is clearly and distinctly perceived. On the other hand, the role the demon plays there need not be the role it plays later in the *Meditations*. And, as a matter of fact, Descartes does later invoke the possibility of the demon's existence as a basis for doubts concerning clear and distinct perceptions. But in the First Meditation the demon has nothing to do with clear and distinct perception for the very good reason that there is no clear and distinct perception in the First Meditation. What, then, *is* the demon's function there?

Two other questions are closely associated with this one. First, what does Descartes accomplish by introducing the demon that he has not already accomplished by the dream argument? Second, if his ground for doubting mathematical truths in the First Meditation is not that even what is clearly and distinctly perceived may be false if there is a demon, what *is* the basis in the First Meditation for his doubts concerning mathematics?

These questions are likely to occur to anyone who focuses his attention on the passage immediately following Descartes's remarks concerning elementary mathematical truths, that "it seems that it cannot be the case that truths so evident should incur any suspicion of falsity." Here is the passage:

Nevertheless there is a certain opinion, long established in my mind, that there is a God who can do everything and by whom I have been created as I am. Now how do I know he has not brought it about that there is no earth at all, no sky, no extended thing, no shape, no size, no place, and that all these things should nevertheless seem to me to exist just as they do now?

The argument of this passage may seem to duplicate the dream argument since it, too, raises doubts about the existence of material things. Moreover, while the context leads the reader to expect the passage to provide a basis for doubting mathematical propositions, the argument in the passage seems as irrelevant to such propositions as does the dream argument. For as Descartes has already observed, arithmetic and geometry "treat only of the simplest and most general things and scarcely care whether those things are in nature or not." Why then does he argue that mathematics is rendered doubtful by the possibility that there is neither earth, nor heaven, nor even very simple and very general things such as extended body, magnitude, and place?

Descartes's argument here does not, as a matter of fact, merely reiterate the same doubts that he raised earlier with the dream argument. For his observation that the distinction between wakefulness and dreaming is uncertain did not affect beliefs in the reality of various simple and universal things—"corporeal nature in general and its extension, the shape of extended things, . . ." and so on. According to the theory of imagination that he invoked in order to account for dreaming, there must be simple and universal things that form the elements of all images and fantasies and that are not themselves invented. The dream argument also left intact the supposition that there *is* a material world: the conclusion Descartes drew from his consideration of dreams was merely that we cannot distinguish with certainty between real material objects and those that are dreamed.

The current passage about an omnipotent deity challenges these two suppositions and therefore goes significantly further than the earlier passage. In particular it raises for the first time the possibility that there are no material objects at all. And it associates this with the possibility, which Descartes has also not previously considered, that even the most simple and universal things are not real.

The fact that Descartes raises these two possibilities in the same breath strongly suggests that they are intimately related: perhaps, he reflects, "there is no earth at all, no sky, no extended thing, no shape, no size." He does not make the relation between the two possibilities explicit, but clarifying it will be useful. Doing so will provide, among other things, a convenient opportunity for clearing up certain difficult aspects of the entire section of the First Meditation that follows the dream argument—difficulties concerning the interpretation of the simples and especially of their existence. What exactly does it mean to assert that the simples are true or that they exist? And just what does Descartes suppose the omnipotent deity is capable of doing when he suggests that God might have arranged that the simples do not exist?

It is easy to be puzzled by these questions. This is particularly so if, as often happens, the doubts raised by the dream argument are erroneously construed as concerning the existence of *all* material objects whatever. For in that case, since Descartes affirms the existence of simples despite the dream argument, it is necessary to understand their existence in such a way that the existence of material objects is irrelevant to it. But the existence of the simples cannot be a matter of the existence of certain ideas, because the omnipotent deity supposedly can arrange that we have ideas of the simples even though they do not exist. It is very mysterious, to say the least, in what sense the nonexistence of the simples can be understood as a function of the nonexistence of matter, given that their nonexistence must be consistent with the occurrence of ideas of simples. After all, what can be done even by an omnipotent being to render our idea of place false, for example, if the truth of the idea is not equivalent to the existence of spatially located objects?

Now the dream argument does *not* cast doubt on the existence of material objects, and once the relevance of this fact is understood, all the difficulties I have mentioned can readily be dispelled in a straightforward manner. The dream argument establishes that the physical world may not include the particular objects that seem to be revealed to our senses, but it does not interfere with the general assumption that there are material, non-imaginary sensory objects. Despite the dream argument, moreover, we can be confident that the characteristics of these material objects include the simple characteristics Descartes enumerates. Complexes of characteristics may be fashioned by our own minds, but we cannot invent the simples themselves. We cannot do so, at least, according to the theory of imagination Descartes propounds after the passage in which he develops the dream argument.

In certain obvious respects this theory parallels Hume's account of ideas.[1] The simples of the First Meditation correspond to the simple ideas Hume says we are incapable of inventing. Simple ideas are derived exclusively from impressions, in Hume's opinion; similarly, the account Descartes gives in the First Meditation starts out

[1] Cf., for instance, Hume's *Enquiry Concerning Human Understanding*, Section II, "Of the Origin of Ideas."

by regarding sensory acquaintance with the simples as the source of our ideas of them. One way in which Descartes differs from Hume is with regard to the question of whether it is possible to distinguish on a sensory basis between impressions and ideas. Hume maintains that it is possible; he believes impressions have greater "force and vivacity" than do ideas. Descartes's dream argument, of course, involves the opposite claim that there is no reliable sensory basis for discriminating between dream images and material objects.

Although the point of the dream argument is that we cannot distinguish between the complex sensory objects of fantasy and those belonging to the material world, the argument does not challenge the assumption that some sensory objects are independent physical existents. We may be unable to identify those of our sensory objects that do exist physically, but it is only through our awareness of these objects that, according to the theory of imagination provisionally invoked by Descartes after the dream argument, we acquire our ideas of the simples. Hence the view Descartes develops in his discussion of the simples is that there really are objects that are corporeal, that have extension, shape, size, and the rest. Otherwise, according to the relevant theory of imagination, we could have no ideas of these simple and universal things. When Descartes says we can be certain that the simples exist, or that our ideas of them are true, what he means is that we can be certain of the existence of material objects whose characteristics include the simple characteristics he enumerates. Our ideas of the simples are true, then, in the sense that there are real objects with the characteristics of which we have ideas. The simples exist in the sense that they characterize real things.

The dream argument challenges the common-sense assumption, which Hume accepts, that there is a sensory difference between dream images and material objects. And when the First Meditation raises the possibility that there is an omnipotent deity, it challenges another doctrine of common sense, also accepted by Hume— namely, the doctrine that all ideas must ultimately be traceable to experience or, in Hume's term, to impressions. For when Descartes considers the possibility that an omnipotent deity exists, it occurs to him that the theories of imagination he has discussed may be false.

Ideas of the most simple and universal things might have been put into our minds by a deity or a demon even if there were no material reality at all. If an omnipotent being had done this, the simples would not exist and our ideas of them would not be true; if there were no heaven or earth, there would be nothing with size or place. The nonexistence of the material world entails the nonexistence of the simples, because the latter exist only as characteristics of the former. This explains how the possibility of an omnipotent being leads Descartes to have doubts about the simple things whose existence was able to survive the dream argument. The import of the dream argument is essentially epistemological: it bears upon our ability to distinguish two sorts of existents—images and material objects. The import of the hypothesis concerning an omnipotent deity, on the other hand, is essentially metaphysical: it bears upon the very existence of matter itself.

But what about the truths of mathematics, which also survived Descartes's discussion of dreaming? They would seem to be no more affected by the argument that neither earth nor sky nor the simples may exist than they were affected by the dream argument. The possibility that there is no physical world appears to be entirely irrelevant to truths such as those of arithmetic or geometry.

The hypothesis that there is an omnipotent being seems, in fact, to lead to doubts about mathematical truths in a way quite different from that in which it leads to doubts concerning the existence of matter and of the simples. After explaining that an omnipotent deity might give us false ideas of simples, Descartes says:

> *And what is more, just as I sometimes judge that others are mistaken about the very things that they consider themselves to know most perfectly, how do I know that God has not brought it about that I am mistaken every time I add two and three together or count the sides of a square or [do something even simpler], if anything simpler can be imagined?*
>
> *And yet, perhaps God willed that I should not be deceived in that fashion, for he is said to be supremely good. But if it should be inconsistent with his goodness to have created me so that I am always mistaken, it would seem no less foreign to his goodness to allow that I should be sometimes mistaken, which, however, cannot be maintained.*

The problem is not that there may be no reality about which to make judgments, but that we may commit errors in the course of arriving at even the most elementary judgments of mathematics. I wish, however, to postpone considering the exact nature of the errors Descartes is contemplating in this passage.

It is plausible to suppose that the omnipotent being accomplishes two distinct tasks in the First Meditation, each task corresponding to one of the two sorts of belief that survive the dream argument. The possibility that we are dreaming does not affect the belief in a material world whose most general and simple characteristics can be known; nor does it affect the truth of mathematical propositions. The first of these beliefs is undermined by the hypothesis that an omnipotent deity may have stocked our imaginations with ideas to which nothing corresponds. The possibility that the deity leads us to make mistakes whenever we think about mathematics undermines the second.

The idea that there may be an omnipotent deity is introduced, then, in order to raise doubts about the beliefs that escape the dream argument. It undermines the beliefs in the existence of a physical world and of the simples through one argument, and confidence in mathematics through another. What is not so clear, however, is whether mathematical judgments are affected only by the second of these arguments, or whether the first has a bearing on them as well. It may seem at first glance that the first argument can have nothing to do with the truth of mathematical judgments. After all, the First Meditation itself seems to point out that the truths of mathematics are independent of any existence. And this seems to entail that those truths are quite unaffected even by the most radical doubts concerning the reality of the world and of the simples.

The trouble with this interpretation, however, is that it conflicts with the fact that mathematical propositions are not clearly and distinctly perceived in the First Meditation. The First Meditation is devoted to beliefs that are thought to be derived "from or through the senses." Since it discusses mathematical propositions, Descartes must be regarding these propositions as somehow based on sensory testimony; he cannot be construing their truth, accordingly, as independent of all questions of existence. Construing them in the latter "pure" manner would require very clear and distinct perception indeed, and it would be inconsistent with the supposition that mathematical judgments are among those that come "from or through the senses."

I have already pointed out that in the *Conversation with Burman* Descartes indicates clearly that he does not suppose any of the general propositions considered in the First Meditation to be understood "in the abstract and separated from matter and from particular instances." He observes, moreover, that in the First

73

Meditation "it is principally a question of an existing thing—that is, whether it exists."[2] There is a genuine basis, therefore, for wondering whether he is, in the First Meditation, supposing that the truth of mathematical judgments is actually independent of all questions of existence.

It is obviously essential to give careful attention to the passage in which Descartes seems to assert this. The passage follows immediately after he makes the claim that, despite the dream argument and despite our capacity to fabricate imaginary things, the simples may be known to characterize all existence. He enumerates these simples, belief in whose existence escapes all the skeptical considerations he has so far advanced, and then says:

> *In the light of these considerations, perhaps we are right to conclude that physics, astronomy, medicine, and all other disciplines that depend on a consideration of composite things are indeed doubtful; and that arithmetic, geometry, and others of that sort, which treat only of the simplest and most general things and scarcely care whether those things are in nature or not, contain something certain and indubitable* [indubitati]. *For whether I am awake or asleep, two and three joined together are five, and a square does not have more than four sides. And it seems that it cannot be the case that truths so evident should incur any suspicion of falsity.*

It is important to be clear about the contrast Descartes draws here between physics, astronomy, and medicine on the one hand and the various branches of mathematics on the other. He does not present it as a contrast between sciences to which existence is relevant and those to which it is not. He presents it primarily as a contrast between sciences that deal with complex existents and those that deal with very simple and general things. The latter sciences are less specialized than the former. But this is because they are concerned with all existents, not because they are concerned with none. The mathematical sciences are supposed to deal with *everything*, not with nothing.

When Descartes begins to consider mathematics, his dream argument has already justified doubts concerning the existence of particular complex objects and his discussion of imagination has justified doubts concerning the existence of objects of particular complex types. Since physics, astronomy, and medicine deal with

---

[2] AT V, 146; Charles Adam, ed., *Entretien avec Burman* (Paris: Boivin, 1937), pp. 4-5.

complex objects, he must regard these sciences as dubious and uncertain. But he has not developed any basis for doubt concerning the assumption that there are some complex physical things. In the passage dealing with the simples, moreover, he has pointed out that it is reasonable to ascribe certain very simple and general characteristics to what exists despite the skeptical arguments he has so far advanced.

Now mathematics deals with these very simple and general characteristics of things, and it is for this reason that it is not concerned with the real existence of any particular complex object. This does not entail, however, that mathematics is not concerned at all with existence. From the statement that mathematics has nothing to do with any particular object or complex sort of object it does not follow that it has nothing whatever to do with existing things. Even if the truth of mathematics is independent of the existence of any particular thing or complex type of thing, it does not follow that mathematics may be true even if nothing whatever exists.

In the First Meditation, Descartes does in fact regard the truth of mathematical judgments as depending upon the existence of things that exhibit the simple characteristics with which he presumes mathematics to deal. He does not suppose that the superior certainty he ascribes to mathematics derives from the indifference of mathematics to all questions of existence, but rather from the ease with which the existential requirements of mathematics may be satisfied. Since *whatever* exists must possess the simple characteristics, mathematics does not depend as other sciences do upon the existence of any specific objects or types of object. What it needs so far as existence goes is provided by the existence of *any* material thing. This is why mathematics is more certain than the other sciences, for the needs of other sciences can be satisfied only by the existence of particular sorts of complex objects, and Descartes has already raised serious doubts about beliefs in their existence.

The text of his discussion of mathematics may appear at first glance to be in conflict with this interpretation, but actually without this interpretation there is difficulty in accounting for the exact text. Descartes says, for instance, that the mathematical sciences deal with very simple and general things and "scarcely care whether those things are in nature or not." But if no questions of existence are relevant to mathematics, why should mathematics care about existence even scarcely? To say that it scarcely cares suggests that it *does* care to some extent, and this would not be so if it did not depend in any way on the existence of anything. Descartes's point is just that since the existence of the simples is established by the existence of anything whatever, it is established *easily* in comparison with the relatively great trouble required to determine the existence of some particular object or type of object.

Another textual consideration is that Descartes's assertion that mathematical truths seem immune to doubt is followed almost immediately by the question: "how do I know he has not brought it about that there is no earth at all, no sky, no extended thing, no shape, no size, no place, and that all these things should nevertheless seem to me to exist just as they do now?" It is apparent that Descartes conceives the possibility he describes in his question as providing a basis for doubting the truth of mathematics. And the possible nonexistence of earth, sky, and the simples would hardly provide such a basis if the truth of mathematics did not depend upon the existence of something.

The truth of mathematics is challenged not only by the observation that neither earth nor sky nor the simples may exist, but also by the additional suggestion that all mathematical judgments may involve the commission of errors. I have postponed considering the exact meaning of this suggestion, but will now try to explain what sort of error Descartes has in mind as constituting a threat to the certainty of mathematical beliefs. It is not very difficult to explain, because Descartes himself discusses an example of error in mathematics.

Curiously, very little attention has been given by students of Descartes to this example. The discussion occurs in the course of his Reply to the Seventh Set of Objections, where his examination of various problems pertaining to the First Meditation leads him to refer to a hypothetical situation his critic had described. He says of this situation: "the example he himself [i.e., the critic] introduced above, about the man who counted one o'clock four times, proves that a person who adds 2 and 3 together can be deceived."[3] What is the example? Descartes's critic, the Jesuit Bourdin, presents it in the following way:

> *I knew a man who once while falling asleep heard a clock strike four and counted this way: one, one, one, one. And then because of the absurdity of the situation he was conceiving he exclaimed:*

[3] HR II, 278; AT VII, 476, ll. 5-8.

"the clock is really going mad. It has struck one o'clock four times!"[4]

The error committed by the man in this example is clearly not a result of defective memory; on the contrary, his error depends upon his recollecting the number of strokes sounded by the clock quite accurately. This is one indication that the unreliability of memory is not what Descartes supposes to threaten mathematical judgments in the First Meditation.

The following point is also worth considering. The thesis that Descartes's confidence in mat: matics is threatened by the unreliability of memory requires the assumption that memory is involved in making *all* judgments. For Descartes says that the danger of deception is present not only in the arithmetical and geometrical judgments that he discusses, but even in simpler ones, "if anything simpler can be imagined." Advocates of the memory thesis must claim, therefore, that the naïve empiricist of the First Meditation believes that the use of memory enters into even the simplest judgments. There may be something to be said for this belief, but it is something that can be said only on the basis of a rather sophisticated epistemological analysis. It is not plausible to suppose that an analysis of this kind plays a role in the First Meditation.[5]

To return to the example Descartes discusses in his Reply to the Seventh Set of Objections, the trouble is that the error it describes seems due more to general confusion than to faulty arithmetic. So far as the counting of the strokes goes, the error committed is not a purely arithmetical mistake, of the sort that a person makes when he adds a column of figures incorrectly or when he suffers a lapse in his grasp of the multiplication tables. The man in the example is less the victim of a blunder than of a misconception. His error may perhaps be regarded as analogous to the mistake made by a person who slips into supposing that the result of adding 2 and 2 is 22, or by a person who, without realizing what he is doing, takes the product of a pair of numbers he is supposed to add instead of taking their sum.

It is not easy to give a precise characterization of the error described in the example, but it is not necessary to insist upon a

---

[4] HR II, 263; AT VII, 457, ll. 8-12.
[5] For a defense of the memory thesis, cf. Doney, "The Cartesian Circle," *Journal of the History of Ideas*, XVI (1955), esp. pp. 329-330. Further criticism of the thesis may be found in my essay, "Memory and the Cartesian Circle," *Philosophical Review*, LXXI (1962), 504-511, and in Chapter 13 below.

definitive formulation of it. For Descartes's point is not that there is some specific type of error that may infect simple mathematical judgments. His point is merely the very general one that a feeling of confidence about an elementary judgment is not an adequate sign that the judgment is true, since even in the simplest matters it is always possible that *something* has gone wrong. There are any number of ways in which something may go wrong, and in the case described in the example the error is a rather bizarre one. The usefulness of the example is not that it provides a paradigm from which one might derive a theory concerning the sort of error to which mathematical judgments are susceptible. Its function, as Descartes explains, is simply that it "proves that a person who adds 2 and 3 together can be deceived."

Descartes's claim that we may be deceived even in simple mathematical judgments is not, then, a claim based on the specific nature of these judgments or on the specific type of evidence that is available to support them. It is based on nothing more elaborate or sophisticated than an awareness that men are susceptible to committing blunders of even the most egregious sort and that they sometimes become confused about even the most transparent matters. Descartes is not relying on a theory that the evidence upon which mathematical judgments may be based is inherently and inescapably inconclusive. His aim is not to call attention to any logical gap in the relation between mathematical judgments and the grounds on which they are affirmed. He is simply calling attention to the well-known propensity of men to settle upon judgments that do not reflect a proper grasp of the material with which they are dealing, but reflect only their own vagaries and misconceptions.

9

DEMONS, DREAMERS, AND MADMEN

Descartes's discussion of the origin of human faculties is, like the earlier portions of his critique of the senses, dialectical. It proceeds from an initial thesis to criticism, to rebuttal, and then to more refined criticism until it reaches its final skeptical outcome. The course of the argument is relatively straightforward, but reviewing its steps will nevertheless be useful.

Immediately after he observes, regarding the elementary propositions of arithmetic and geometry, that "it seems that it cannot be the case that truths so evident should incur any suspicion of falsity," Descartes recognizes that it is in fact possible to doubt these propositions on the basis of the notion that there is "a God who can do everything and by whom I have been created as I am." I have already pointed out that Descartes thinks there are two ways in which he might be deceived about even the simplest things. The hypothesis that his creator made him defective in these two ways is the first thesis in the dialectic of his argument.

This thesis is immediately criticized on the ground that, according to the accepted view, God is good and his goodness may be incompatible with his having created men in such a way that they are constantly deceived. It is not certain that God's goodness is incompatible with his being a deceiver, however, and Descartes proceeds to rebut the objection he has raised against the original thesis by developing a brief argument designed to show that deception and goodness are not actually incompatible. This argument starts with his observation that he is in fact sometimes deceived; the fact that deception occurs at all, he then argues, shows that it cannot be incompatible with divine goodness. And if deception and divine goodness are compatible, it is possible after all that God has created men in such a way that they are constantly deceived. The original thesis may therefore be correct.

The argument Descartes uses to rebut the objection to his original thesis is of very dubious value, and he himself does not regard it as sound. One of its questionable aspects is its assumption that if it is compatible with God's goodness that we are sometimes deceived, then it must also be compatible with his goodness that we are always deceived. In the Sixth Meditation Descartes shows that this assumption is incorrect; he argues there that while our always being deceived is incompatible with divine goodness, our sometimes being deceived is not. Here in the First Meditation, however, the relatively naïve and unphilosophical inquirer whose role he plays is not in a position to recognize that his argument is unsound. He has no clear understanding of the nature of God and he is therefore persuaded by an argument which has only a certain prima facie plausibility.

Descartes presents the argument in a tentative manner, with plain textual indications that the inquirer of the First Meditation is not confident of it. Thus the text reads: "But if it should be inconsistent with his goodness to have created me so that I am always mistaken, it would seem no less foreign to his goodness to allow that I should be sometimes mistaken." This appearance is illusory, but the level of sophistication Descartes's inquirer has attained at this point in his philosophical development is not sufficient to enable him to see through it. Descartes represents him, however, as uncertain; it is not clear to him whether or not the appearance of validity is to be credited. He cannot tell which view of the relation between divine goodness and deception is reasonable, and therefore cannot decide whether or not the hypothesis that God has arranged for us to be constantly deceived is a reasonable one. In other words, he is not sure whether or not he has reasonable grounds for doubting the elementary beliefs whose certainty is at stake. If God can deceive us constantly, then the inquirer has a reasonable ground for doubt; if not, then he does not. And he is not in a position to decide between these alternatives.

For all that Descartes knows in the First Meditation, the common opinion that there is a God provides a reasonable ground for doubting even the simplest things. But just as he is unable to comprehend clearly the nature of God and its implications for human knowledge, he is also in no position to decide whether believing in the existence of God is itself reasonable. After observing that for all he knows God may arrange for him to be constantly deceived, he raises the possibility that there may not actually be a God with the power to render him incapable of knowledge. Descartes does not attempt to refute the position of atheists or of those who deny God's omnipotence. He attempts instead to show that similar doubts about the competence of the human mind are also reasonable even if men are not created by an omnipotent deity.

His argument is that there is even more reason to suspect that the human mind is defective if its origin lies in a source less powerful than God. Since the tendency to make mistakes is a defect, he points out, the mind is more likely to err if it is the product of a less competent or trustworthy maker. There are several possible origins of the human mind other than God: the mind may have arisen by chance, or it may have been fated that men should be as they are, or human nature may be entirely due to a series of natural causes. None of these alternatives seems to Descartes to exclude the possibility that the human mind is inherently defective and subject to continual error.

Descartes's argument here has the form of a constructive dilemma: either the human mind is the work of an omnipotent God or it is not; if it is the work of God, then it may be defective; if it is not the work of God, then it may be defective; therefore, the human mind may be defective. No resolution of this dilemma is possible in the First Meditation because Descartes does not clearly understand the relation between the nature of God and human nature. The inadequacy of his understanding at this stage is revealed by the fact that he is inclined to accept a proposition he later shows to be incorrect—the proposition that God's goodness is compatible with men being constantly deceived.

Several points in Descartes's discussion of the origin of the human mind call for particular attention. I will mention them briefly, then consider them in greater detail. First, the doubt Descartes's argument supports is universal in scope. At any rate, its scope is as great as that of the First Meditation itself: no type of proposition considered there escapes the doubt that the argument generates. Second, Descartes completes his argument and engenders this universal doubt without mentioning the *malin génie*. Third, the conclusion that Descartes reaches in his argument is relevant to the possibility that he may himself be insane—a possibility that he raised earlier in the First Meditation and peremptorily rejected.

Descartes introduces the doubts aroused by a consideration of his origin in a discussion of mathematical propositions, but these doubts are not confined to propositions of this sort. Confusion and misconception are not uniquely indigenous to mathematical contexts; they may lead to erroneous judgments of any kind. Hence taking them into account supports not merely a doubt about mathematics but a concern that error may be ubiquitous in human judgment. It undermines confidence even in the simplest judgments, but not only in these; it gives rise to doubts that are quite universal in scope. This is also true of the other sort of doubt Descartes derives from the hypothesis that our natures may be defective. As I have shown, the possibility that the simples do not exist supports a doubt about the assumption upon which the truth of mathematics is supposed to rest. Since the judgments in which Descartes is interested in his critique of the senses all concern the existence of complexes that are composed of simples, the same assumption is required for the truth of *any* judgment whose acceptability he considers in the First Meditation. Unlike the doubts he raises at earlier stages of his inquiry, moreover, these doubts contemplate the possibility that *all* judgments may be false. What Descartes fears is no longer merely that he cannot distinguish satisfactorily between true and false judgments, but that none of his judgments is true.

It is not necessary for him to invoke an omnipotent deity in order to provide a basis for such doubts. Ideas of nonexistent simples might come into our minds by chance or from natural causes; and surely no supernatural being need be hypothesized in order to establish the possibility that human judgment is continually beset by confusion and misconception. But while the supposition that a supernatural being exists is not necessary in order to raise the doubts at issue, it *is* necessary in order to *eliminate* them. If, as Descartes claims, the human mind is the more likely to be defective as its origin is the less exalted, only the most exalted origin possible can guarantee its freedom from all defect. Only the supposition that men are created by a deity who is incapable of producing something defective can provide a conclusive reason for denying that they are doomed to error by their very nature. Any other account of human origin is consistent with the assumption that men's minds are defective, and thus provides a basis for doubt.

At an earlier stage of the First Meditation Descartes peremptorily dismissed all doubts about his sanity and completely ignored the possible influence upon his beliefs of certain other abnormalities. I defended the legitimacy of this procedure on the ground that the nature of his inquiry required him to assume an ideally qualified inquirer: it would have been unreasonable, my defense ran, for

Descartes to begin by entertaining doubts concerning defects that would render him incapable of attaining certainty. But if Descartes could properly dismiss or ignore those earlier doubts, why should he take these later ones seriously? If he was justified in refusing to consider the possibility that he might be mad or color blind, why is he not equally justified in dismissing the possibility that his mind is defective in the ways suggested by the hypothesis that there is an omnipotent deity?

Descartes's failure to dismiss this possibility seems particularly curious in view of the striking similarity between madness on the one hand and the defects he discusses in connection with the hypothetical deity on the other. A madman lives in his own world, which has reality only within his mind; but so do we all if our ideas of the simples correspond to nothing real. The judgment of a madman is confused and dominated by misconceptions which direct it to bizarre errors; but this is precisely what Descartes envisages when he suggests that we may be deceived in all our judgments. If our ideas of the simples correspond to nothing real, or if our judgment is invariably distorted by confusion and misconception, then, it seems, we *are* insane. At any rate, we seem no more capable of distinguishing what is reasonable from what is unreasonable than do those whom we generally identify as mad.

There is nevertheless an important difference between these defects and insanity. Insanity differentiates some men from others and makes them peculiarly unsuited to conduct a rational inquiry. The defects whose possibility Descartes entertains here, on the other hand, are not supposed to be idiosyncratic; they are supposed to characterize the human mind as such. The problem to which the *Meditations* is devoted is how, if at all, certainty can be attained by those who are best qualified to pursue it. For this reason Descartes properly supposes himself free of all defects or deficiencies that would render him less qualified than others to conduct the inquiry. But he does not, of course, suppose that he is exempt from incapacities uniformly affecting all human minds. The defects on whose possibility his doubts concerning mathematical judgments rest are not individual peculiarities; they are implicit in the way men are made and characteristic of human minds generally. The argument that justified dismissing the possibility of insanity as not germane to the inquiry does not, accordingly, apply to the possibility of these defects.

Another aspect of this matter must also be taken seriously into account. Descartes cannot decide whether his origin is in chance, or in nature, or in some supernatural being. Moreover, he cannot decide whether or not an omnipotent being would be capable of making him in such a way that he is constantly deceived. It is not clear to him which of these alternatives is the most reasonable to accept. Now if it should ultimately turn out that he does find a way of deciding among these alternatives, and if it should also turn out that the alternative which he is led to decide upon entails the possibility or actuality that human nature is inherently defective, what will this signify? It will signify that the enterprise of rational inquiry has defeated itself. It will mean that when inquiry is conducted in the most reasonable manner it leads to the conclusion that no reasonable inquiry can be conducted. The question left open at the close of Descartes's discussion of the origin of human nature in the First Meditation, therefore, is the question of whether the assumption that rational inquiry is possible reduces itself to absurdity.

Descartes cannot answer this question yet because he cannot determine whether his origin is in nature, in chance, or in a supernatural being. Moreover, he cannot determine the characteristics of a supernatural being and their implications for the character of the human mind. To a considerable extent the later argument of the *Meditations* is devoted to settling these questions. The problem left by Descartes's argument in the First Meditation may be formulated in this way: Is it reasonable to believe that rational inquiry is possible, or does proceeding in the most reasonable way lead us to conclude either that rational inquiry is not possible because the human mind is inherently defective, or that its possibility must remain in doubt because we cannot reasonably decide between various alternative propositions that are relevant to the question of its possibility?

The negative outcome of Descartes's argument in the First Meditation does not require his resort to supernatural agencies. He uses the possibility that there is a deity to introduce a general doubt, but does not actually assume that the legitimacy of this doubt depends upon his hypothesis about God. He himself points out that, on the contrary, the doubt is stronger without the supposition that there is a deity. The assumption that God does *not* exist—the assumption that "all this regarding God is fictitious"—provides an even better reason for general doubt than its alternative does. Not only does God play no essential role in establishing the skeptical outcome of the First Meditation, but neither does the *malin génie.* The supposition that there is a demon supports no additional doubts beyond those that Descartes has already engendered prior to introducing it. The skeptical argument of the First Meditation is, in fact, complete by the time Descartes introduces the demon.

After the affirmation of general skepticism to which his discussion of mathematics has led him, Descartes says: "But it is not yet enough to have observed these things; I must be careful to bear them in mind." Despite his having shown that all the beliefs he has examined are doubtful, there is a danger that his reason will be overcome by the force of habit and that discredited opinions will occupy his mind "even entirely against my will." Descartes regards this risk as particularly great because while he has shown that the beliefs in question are doubtful, they are "nonetheless highly probable—opinions that it is far more reasonable to believe than to deny." In order to overcome his inclination to continue believing what is only probable, Descartes resolves to "pretend for a while" that all these beliefs are entirely false. He hopes in this way to arrange that the scales of his judgment are "balanced with prejudices on both sides."

This is how the demon comes into the picture. Descartes postulates its existence in order to support the "pretense" that all the beliefs at issue are not simply doubtful but false. And it is this that leads Henri Gouhier to observe that the idea of the demon "n'a aucune signification métaphysique; c'est un artifice purement méthodologique qui permet au doute de continuer. . . ."[1] The assumption that the demon exists is not introduced in order to provide a basis for doubting things that are left undoubted in the preceding discussion. It is supposed, rather, to refresh doubts whose legitimacy has already been established. Thus Gouhier explains that

> *cet ultime argument affermit les précédents et les défend contre la sollicitation humble, insinuante et tenace du vraisemblable; s'il n'est pas la première raison qui m'oblige à me méfier des sensations, il est celle qui m'oblige à persévérer dans cette méfiance.*[2]

In Gouhier's view Descartes needs the demon only in order to invigorate his ability to doubt matters that he has already shown to be uncertain but that continue nonetheless to tempt his assent:

---

[1] Henri Gouhier, *Essais sur Descartes* (Paris: J. Vrin, 1949), p. 154.
[2] *Ibid.*, pp. 152-153.

Un soupçon métaphysiquement fondé n'a qu'une efficacité vite usée. A mesure que les vérités tombent, elles se relèvent métamorphosées en probabilités: je crois plutot à la réalité des choses qu'à une illusion de mon esprit; je crois plutot à l'absence d'une tromperie originelle qu'à l'hypothèse contraire. Le malin génie biffe ces "plutot" en rétablissant l'équilibre par un pessimisme radical qui rend également probables les solutions pratiquement abandonnées.[3]

This interpretation is rather plausible, and there is truth in it. But that it is not entirely correct is not difficult to show. Descartes does not use the hypothesis that there is a demon merely to restore a balance of probabilities or to reestablish an equilibrium between what he believes by custom and what he has shown to be doubtful. Nor is it quite accurate to say, as Gouhier does, that the demon serves to enable his doubts to continue.

For the hypothesis that there is a demon does not in fact lead to a reaffirmation by Descartes of the *doubtfulness* of the judgments he considers in the First Meditation, but rather to the affirmation that these judgments are *false.* The demon hypothesis does not simply refresh his awareness that he may be deceived in all the judgments at issue; it entails that he is deceived in all of them. Descartes does not limit himself merely to entertaining the demon's existence as a possibility or to suggesting that a demon may perhaps be deceiving him. He affirms the existence of the demon and the occurrence of the deception: "I will suppose, therefore ... some evil spirit who is supremely powerful and cunning and who has expended all his energy in deceiving me."

The passage in which Descartes first mentions the demon is certainly concerned, as Gouhier suggests, with supporting doubts whose vigor may falter, and thus Gouhier is partly correct in what he says. But there are two respects in which his interpretation is not altogether accurate. First of all, the assumption that there is a demon has certain logical effects on the course of Descartes's argument. Earlier in the First Meditation, Descartes transformed his assertion that he might possibly be dreaming into a postulate: "suppose," he said, "that we *are* dreaming." His postulate concerning the demon affects his subsequent argument in the same way that his earlier postulate concerning dreaming did. It provides a condition his argument must thenceforth take into account, and it poses a problem he must solve if he is to avoid skepticism.

[3] *Ibid.*, pp. 153-154.

Moreover, Gouhier is not correct when he speaks as though the passage in which Descartes first mentions the demon is the first in which the demon appears. For in the earlier passage concerning the origin of his mind, Descartes raised the possibility that there is a supernatural being with the power and the will to deceive him. He did not at that time identify this being as a demon; he referred to it, rather, as a God. But it is the same being that he later describes as a *malin génie*. And this being, however designated, certainly does serve a metaphysical function. It is not introduced merely to refresh old doubts whose vigor is failing, but to provide a basis for doubts that had not previously been entertained at all.

Part 2

REASON
AND ITS VALIDATION

The epidemic doubt generated in the First Meditation is arrested early in the Second, when Descartes discovers in his own existence a belief that is apparently immune to even the most virulent skepticism. This discovery (and the statement *cogito ergo sum* that is widely associated with it) has been the subject of innumerable glosses, commentaries, and interpretations. Philosophers and non-philosophical writers have often detached it from its connection to the rest of Descartes's work in order to explore its significance more freely. I shall deal with it, however, only as an episode in the progress of the inquiry that Descartes undertakes in the *Meditations*.

Descartes begins the Second Meditation with a brief review of the position to which he has so far been led. Then he asks a new question: "I myself, am I not at least something?" He thinks for the first time of himself, having previously focused his attention exclusively on the objects of his awareness. And he is struck by the possibility that in thinking of himself he has come across a belief that the arguments of the First Meditation do not render uncertain. He formulates this belief only in the vaguest way: "I am something," or *sum*. But without first seeking to make it more precise or more explicit, he proceeds to confront it with the grounds for doubt that he has already developed in his examination of sensory beliefs.

There are four steps in Descartes's discussion of *sum*, following the question with which he begins:

I myself, am I not at least something?

a) But I have already denied that I have any senses or a body. Yet I am perplexed, for what follows from that? Am I so tied to a body and to senses that without them I cannot be?

b) But I have persuaded myself that there is nothing at all in the world—no heaven, no earth, no minds, no bodies. Have I not, therefore, also persuaded myself that I am not? By no means. Surely, if I persuaded myself of anything, I was.

c) But there is a consummately powerful and crafty deceiver of some sort who assiduously deceives me at all times. Then if he deceives me, there is no doubt that I am. And let him deceive me as much as he can, still he will never bring it about that I am nothing as long as I think that I am something.

d) Hence now that more thorough consideration has been given to the matter, it must finally be concluded that this proposition: I am, I exist, is necessarily true as often as it is uttered by me or conceived by my mind.[1]

What Descartes says in this passage is clearly related to his famous dictum, *cogito ergo sum;* the passage has been described, indeed, as "Descartes's formulation of the *cogito* in the Second Meditation."[2] But the passage consists of a number of different statements, and *none* of them is the *cogito*. The statement, *I think, therefore I am*, simply does not occur in the passage at all; and neither does any exactly equivalent statement. In fact, the *cogito* as such does not appear anywhere in the *Meditations*. I propose to take Descartes's text on its own terms and to approach it without preconceptions based on the speculation that *cogito ergo sum* adequately formulates its meaning.

Descartes does make a statement in the course of his discussion of *sum* that clearly resembles the *cogito*. This statement occurs in the second step of his argument, along the way to the conclusion, when he asserts that his existence is rendered certain by the fact that he has thought of something. It seems clear to me, for reasons I shall give later on, that in this step and elsewhere Descartes regards his existence as something he infers rather than something that is self-evident to him. The purpose of his inference, however, is not to prove that *sum* is true. One indication of this is that Descartes's argument does not terminate, as it might naturally have done if its intent was to establish the truth of *sum*, with the affirma-

[1] HR I, 150; AT VII, 24, l. 24—25, l. 13. I will give no further citations for quotations from this passage.

[2] Jaako Hintikka, "*Cogito Ergo Sum* as an Inference and a Performance," *Philosophical Review*, LXXII (1963), 490. My essay, "Descartes's Discussion of his Existence in the Second Meditation," *Philosophical Review*, LXXV (1966), offers a critique of the interpretation offered by Hintikka in this article and an earlier one: "*Cogito Ergo Sum:* Inference or Performance?" *Philosophical Review*, LXXI (1962).

tion of his existence in (*b*). The argument continues until it reaches another conclusion in its final step. My analysis of this conclusion suggests that his concern is not to decide whether or not he exists, or to offer a proof of *sum*, but to establish that his existence is in a rather unusual sense certain or indubitable. I shall attempt to clarify the significance of his conclusion about his existence, and to illuminate the intent of his inquiry, by following the dialectical development of his views through the four steps of his argument.

The first ground for doubt with which Descartes confronts *sum* is the supposition, at which he arrived in the First Meditation, that he has neither senses nor a body. Interestingly enough, this confrontation is inconclusive; Descartes does not know what to make of the logical relation between his supposition and *sum:*

> *a*) *But I have already denied that I have any senses or a body. Yet I am perplexed, for what follows from that? Am I so tied to a body and to senses that without them I cannot be?*

It is unclear to him what his supposition implies, if anything, as to his existence. He is perplexed; he cannot decide whether the nonexistence of his senses and his body constitutes a reasonable basis for doubting that he is "something."

It is easy to understand why Descartes is puzzled, for his conception of his own nature at this stage is vague to the point of vacuity. Some of the difficulties in comprehending his discussion of *sum* and his subsequent analysis of his nature derive, indeed, from the fact that his discussion of his existence must contribute as much to developing an understanding of "I" as to determining the acceptability of *sum*. Descartes cannot deal with the belief that he exists without broaching the question of *what* he is. It is to be expected, then, that the views he subsequently develops about his nature will be foreshadowed in the course of his examination of *sum*. It is a problem of very great interest to evaluate the legitimacy of the way in which he handles this matter. I shall postpone considering this problem, however, until the next chapter and for the present, limit my attention to elucidating the passage (*a*)–(*d*).

Questions about existence require, in general, some nonvacuous description of what it is whose existence is being questioned. Since Descartes thinks of himself only as a "something," he is understandably unable to discern the logical relation between the proposition that he exists and the supposition that he has no body or senses. He cannot cope with the question of whether *sum* is undermined by this supposition because coping with it requires a fuller understanding of his own nature than he is currently able to command.

It is noteworthy, therefore, that in the next step he copes in quite a direct and decisive manner with a question that seems to be of an essentially similar kind. In (*b*) he recalls having been persuaded in the First Meditation that there are no real things at all, neither physical nor mental. And when he asks whether reaching this conclusion was tantamount to being persuaded of his own nonexistence, he answers with no hesitation whatever: "By no means. Surely if I persuaded myself of anything, I was." Now this answer is the closest thing to *cogito ergo sum* in his entire discussion. Without altering its significance in any substantial way, it may in fact be rewritten as "I thought, therefore I existed," which differs from the classical formula only in tense.

Because of its resemblance to the *cogito*, there is a special interest in clarifying Descartes's final statement in (*b*) and its role in his examination of the belief that he exists. The first problem is to account for his ability to grasp so straightforwardly the relation between his existence and the supposition recalled in (*b*), despite the fact that he is unable to decide in (*a*) how the belief that he exists is related to the supposition he considers there. The critical difference between the two steps must lie in the suppositions with which he confronts *sum*, but exactly what is the relevant difference?

The supposition Descartes considers in (*a*) has to do with the nonexistence of various things, while in (*b*) he attends to the fact that he was persuaded or thought of something. Thus there is a conspicuous difference in the content of the suppositions that figure in his first two steps. This difference, however, does not account for his ability to cope readily in the second step with a matter that is beyond his grasp in the first. After all, why should it be easier for him to discern the logical relation between *sum* and a statement about his thinking (or mind) than to discern the relation between *sum* and a statement about his body?

He decides later in the *Meditations*, to be sure, that mind is essential to him whereas body is logically irrelevant to his existence. This doctrine would be relevant to the problem I am now considering if Descartes drew a conclusion about his existence in (*b*) but maintained in (*a*) that no such conclusion is warranted; for that could be explained on the basis of the different logical relationships between himself and his mind on the one hand, and himself and his body on the other. In fact, however, he does not claim in (*a*) that his supposition does not entail *sum*. On the contrary, he is at a loss in (*a*) to understand the relation between the two beliefs.

It is not because he starts from body rather than from mind that Descartes cannot, in (*a*), see either that a conclusion about his existence is warranted or that it is not. When he passes in (*b*) from "I persuaded myself of something" to "I existed," the logic of the transition is no different than if he had derived "I exist" from "I have a body." The one transition is no more problematical than the other. In each case the mere fact of predication suffices to make the transition legitimate; the content of the predication plays no essential role. The transitions are straightforward inferences of the form "B(a) implies (∃x)(x =a)."

Thus the critical difference between (*a*) and (*b*) is formal rather than substantive. Descartes's denial that he has either a body or senses is not a predication such as "I have the property of being bodiless and without senses." If it were, his hesitation would be unaccountable; for "I exist" follows as directly from this statement as "I existed" does from "I thought of something." His supposition in (*a*) is equivalent to "If there are bodies and I do exist, then no body is related to me in such a way as to be mine." Descartes ascribes no property to himself when he makes this statement and therefore he in no way commits himself to an affirmation of his own existence.

In any event Descartes has not yet developed, at this stage of his inquiry, the doctrine he later propounds concerning the logical connections between himself on the one hand and his mind and his body on the other. He no more knows whether he can exist without a mind than he knows whether he can exist without a body, and it would be anachronistic to invoke his metaphysical theory of the self to explain his hesitation in (*a*) or his lack of hesitation in (*b*). The only considerations upon which he relies for his conclusion in (*b*)are formal, and they have nothing particularly to do with minds or with bodies.

This is confirmed by his response to a remark made by Gassendi. Gassendi attempts to denigrate the special interest of the *cogito* by suggesting that Descartes might just as well have inferred his existence from some activity other than thinking, "since it is known by the natural light that whatever acts is."[3] Although Descartes rejects this suggestion, he accepts Gassendi's logical point. He insists that there is a vital difference between the *cogito* and an inference like "I walk, hence I exist"; but he locates this difference in the premisses of the two inferences rather than in their logical structures,

[3] HR II, 137; AT VII, 259, ll. 4-5.

which he concedes to be the same. The peculiarity of the *cogito*, he maintains, lies in the fact that "there is no action of mine of which I am entirely certain ([I mean] of course with that metaphysical certainty which is all that is at issue here) except only of thinking."[4] Deriving *sum* from *cogito* is superior to deriving it from *ambulo*, but only because *ambulo* does not enjoy the metaphysical certitude that characterizes *cogito*.

There are two further pieces of evidence that bear on the character of the derivation in (*b*). Descartes is explicitly concerned with inference in (*a*), where he asks what "follows" from the supposition he considers there. It is plausible to read (*b*) as continuing the pattern of inquiry in (*a*) and, accordingly, to understand the second step as similarly concerned with what follows from the supposition with which it begins. Near the end of the Second Meditation, moreover, Descartes says: "it certainly follows . . . clearly that I myself exist from the fact that I see [this piece of wax]." This too suggests that he regards his existence as something that is inferred.

But just what is the nature of Descartes's inference when he derives his existence from his thinking? One theory is that in the *cogito*, and accordingly in (*b*) as well, his argument is actually an enthymeme: when he moves from a statement about his thinking to a statement about his existence, he relies upon an unexpressed general principle that connects thinking and existing and that serves as a major premiss in his argument. It will be useful to consider this theory, which Descartes himself discusses in several places.

The following passage in *Principles of Philosophy* suggests that a general principle is involved as a premiss in Descartes's transitions from assertions concerning thinking to assertions concerning existing:

> *When I said that this proposition:* I think, therefore I am, *is of all* [propositions] *the first and the most certain that occurs to anyone who philosophizes in an orderly way, I did not thereby deny that one must first know what thought is, what existence is, what certainty is, and know that it cannot be that what thinks does not exist, and such matters. But because these are the simplest notions, which by themselves provide knowledge of no existing things, I did not judge that they had to be taken into account.*[5]

Descartes seems to claim in this passage that the transition can only

---

[4] HR II, 207; AT VII, 352, ll. 8-11.
[5] *Principles of Philosophy*, Part I, sec. x; HR I, 222; AT VIII, 8, ll. 8-16.

be made if he assumes as a premiss the principle that "it cannot be that what thinks does not exist"; and that because it is extremely simple and involves no affirmation of existence, it is proper for him to accept this principle without first discussing whether it is indubitable. Elsewhere, however, he seems to deny that the principle plays any such role:

> *Even when someone says,* I think, therefore I am, or exist, *he does not deduce existence from thinking by means of a syllogism but recognizes it in a simple mental vision* [mentis intuitu] *as if it were a thing known* per se. *This is apparent from the fact that if he deduced it by means of a syllogism he would first have to know this major premise:* everything that thinks is, or exists; *and yet he really learns that rather from what he experiences in himself—that it cannot be the case that he thinks, unless he exists. For the nature of our mind is such that it forms general propositions out of a knowledge of particulars.*[6]

Here Descartes apparently denies that he needs to know any general principle before he can derive his existence from his thinking.

The contradiction between these two passages was called to Descartes's attention during his lifetime. In the *Conversation with Burman,* Burman refers to the second passage and then asks whether the contrary thesis is not found in the first. Descartes's reply to Burman's question is as follows:

> *One can know the major premise:* whatever thinks, is—*before the conclusion* I think, therefore I am; *for in fact it is prior to my conclusion and my conclusion depends upon it. Thus the author says in the* Principles *that it precedes* [the conclusion], *for implicitly it is always presupposed and precedes it. But it is not a consequence that I always expressly and explicitly recognize that it precedes; and I know my conclusion first for I attend only to what I experience in myself—for example,* "I think, therefore I am." *I do not, however, attend in the same way to the general notion* whatever thinks, is. *As I have pointed out before, we do not separate those* [general] *propositions from individual* [instances] *but we consider them in those* [instances]. *It is in this sense that the words you cite should be understood.*[7]

Part of what Descartes has in mind here is that while the general principle *whatever thinks, is* (*or exists*) is logically prior to the

---

[6] HR II, 38; AT VII, 140, l. 20—141, l. 2.

[7] Charles Adam, ed., *Entretien avec Burman* (Paris: Boivin, 1937), pp. 6-7; AT V, 147.

particular statement *I think, therefore I am*, the latter comes first in the order of inquiry or discovery; for "the nature of our mind is such that it forms general propositions out of a knowledge of particulars." Thus a person arrives at a knowledge of the general principle only by discovering in himself the specific connection between his own thinking and his own existing.

It does not suffice, however, to carry the explanation only this far. To do so makes it seem that Descartes must regard knowledge of the general principle as quite superfluous to his inference from thinking to existing. For knowledge of the principle can be derived only from an awareness in a particular case of the connection between thinking and existing, and this awareness is (since the case is his own) already sufficient for him to derive his existence from his thinking. What Descartes says in the second of the passages I have quoted above tends to encourage this way of understanding him. But an interpretation of this sort does not fit either his statements in the passage quoted above from the *Principles* or his defense of those statements in the passage from the *Conversation with Burman*. It is plainly inaccurate to say that Descartes speaks in the *Principles* of the order of logical priority but that he speaks in the other passage of the order of inquiry or discovery. The fact is that he does not, in the *Principles*, say merely that the general principle is logically prior; he says that *we must know it first*. In other words, he says that the principle is first *both* in the order of logic *and* in the order of discovery.

The key to a solution of the difficulty is that Descartes does not regard knowledge of the particular statement as neatly separable from knowledge of the general principle. What the individual learns from his own case is that unless he exists he cannot think. What he knows in his own case is not merely that he both thinks and exists (which would be quite compatible with the falsity of the general principle) but that his thinking *necessarily* involves his existence. Precisely because he perceives the connection as a necessary one, he understands that it must hold generally and not only in the single instance he happens to be considering. Since he understands that the connection between thinking and existing in his own case is a necessary connection, he cannot avoid grasping the general principle that thinking requires existing. But he need not expressly formulate the principle or pay any attention to it. It is "implicitly presupposed," but it plays no active role and need not be explicitly invoked.

Although the premiss from which Descartes derives his existence in (*b*) is "I thought of something," he acknowledges in his exchange with Gassendi that any other premise of the form "B(a)" yields a similar conclusion. The special interest of inferences to existence from thought must, then, reside in the peculiar character of their premises rather than in their logical structures. Now the explanation of this character that Descartes gives to Gassendi—in terms of the "metaphysical certitude" of *cogito*—is misleading. It does not do justice to the unique logical status of *sum*, and it obscures the radical import of the conclusion about his existence that Descartes reaches in (*d*). In order to develop a more adequate appreciation of the matter, I shall first explicate what Descartes does in the final two steps of his argument, then consider the significance of his conclusion and attempt to formulate the insight concerning the indubitability of *sum* in which his discussion culminates.

Of the grounds for doubt that Descartes develops in the First Meditation, the strongest and most inclusive is the supposition that there is a demon of great power who is bent on deception. Following the statement in (*b*) that he existed, Descartes confronts his belief with this demon:

> *c) But there is a consummately powerful and crafty deceiver of some sort who assiduously deceives me at all times. Then if he deceives me, there is no doubt that I am. And let him deceive me as much as he can, he will never bring it about that I am nothing as long as I think that I am something.*

In this step of his inquiry Descartes recalls his notion that there is a demon trying to deceive him, and then he makes two further statements: (i) "if he deceives me, there is no doubt that I am," and (ii) "let him deceive me as much as he can, he will never bring it about that I am nothing as long as I think that I am something."

Descartes does not proceed by describing some specific means by which the demon might try to deceive him and by then showing that an effort of this sort would be bound to fail. Instead, he reduces to absurdity the hypothesis that he can be deceived in believing that he exists. To be deceived, a person must believe or think something erroneously; and (i) asserts that if he believes or thinks something erroneously then he exists. In the special case of the belief that he exists, Descartes would be deceived only if he believed *sum* while *sum* is false—that is, while he is nonexistent; and (ii) asserts that the occurrence of this situation is logically impossible. Not even an omnipotent demon can arrange for Descartes to believe erroneously that he exists, for he cannot be deceived without existing.

What Descartes says in (c) lends itself readily to formulation as the following *reductio ad absurdum:*

1. *I am deceived in thinking that I exist.*
2. *If I am deceived about anything, then I exist.*
3. *Hence, if I am deceived in thinking that I exist, then I do exist.*
4. *Therefore I do exist.*
5. *If I do exist, then I am not deceived in thinking that I exist.*
6. *Therefore, I am not deceived in thinking that I exist.*

It seems clear that this argument fairly represents Descartes's intention in (c). The argument shows that he cannot reasonably doubt *sum*, by showing that there is a contradiction in supposing that *sum* is falsely believed.

It may be noted that (c) involves a shift in tense. Descartes infers in (b) that he existed at the time, during the first of his meditations, when he persuaded himself that there is no heaven, no earth, and so on. But he does not invoke the demon to threaten this belief; in (c), he does not refer to "I existed" but to "I exist." It is fairly simple to explain this shift, which has little philosophical significance. Descartes's use of the past tense in (b) arises out of the narrative mode of his discourse in the *Meditations,* which recounts what transpired during a series of meditations taking place on successive days. It occurs to him early in the second of these meditations that what happened yesterday entails that he existed then. But he is not especially interested in his existence at any particular time, and when he shifts to the present tense in (c) it is best to understand him as concerned with developing a generalized or tenseless account of the belief that he exists. His affirmation in (b) concerning his past existence is due merely to the literary or pedagogical strategy that he adopts in the *Meditations,* it seems to me, and reflects no analytical necessities of his inquiry.

Descartes's discussion concludes with a characterization of *sum.* Since his discussion begins with the question of whether he exists, it might have been expected to end with an answer to this question —that is, with an assertion or denial of *sum* or, perhaps, with an assertion or denial that *sum* is certain. Instead, however, the final outcome of the discussion is a characterization of *sum* as "necessarily true as often as it is uttered by me or conceived by my mind."

Just what is Descartes saying here about *sum?* It is apparent that he is not calling it a necessary truth in the familiar logical sense. A proposition is necessarily true in this sense if its denial is self-contradictory; but the denial of *sum* is not a formal contradiction.

Moreover, logical properties do not come and go. If what Descartes had in mind was necessary truth in the logical sense, it would be absurd for him to specify, as he does, the times when *sum* is necessarily true.

His conclusion *can* appropriately be formulated as an ascription of logically necessary truth to a certain proposition, but that proposition is not *sum*. It is the proposition that *sum* is true whenever he utters or conceives it. His conclusion is, in other words, that it is logically impossible for him to utter or to conceive *sum* without *sum* being true. This conclusion in no way denies, of course, that *sum* is logically contingent. When he describes *sum* as necessarily true on certain occasions, he does not mean that on those occasions it possesses the logical property of necessary truth. He means that it is a logically necessary truth that *sum* is true on those occasions. The following statement from *Principles of Philosophy* tends to confirm this way of understanding his conclusion: "It does not follow that we who think . . . are nothing, for it is *inconsistent* to suppose that what thinks does not exist at the same time as it thinks."[8]

It will be easier to appreciate the role in Descartes's inquiry of his conclusion about *sum* if care is taken to distinguish it from several other statements that are rather similar to it. In the first place, then, his conclusion is not that *sum* is true whenever he is thinking, or that his thinking entails his existing. Despite the fact that the *cogito* does not occur in the Second Meditation, readers may feel a strong inclination to suppose that Descartes's examination of the question of his existence *must* culminate, regardless of the language he uses, in his most famous insight. But his conclusion does not, as the *cogito* does, concern thinking in general. It concerns uttering *sum* or conceiving it. Thus his conclusion cannot be regarded as equivalent to *cogito ergo sum*.

Second, since uttering a proposition or conceiving it in one's mind are not the same as asserting or believing it, Descartes's conclusion is not that *sum* is necessarily true whenever it is believed. No doubt Descartes realized that *sum* cannot be believed falsely, but this is not his conclusion. What he evidently has in mind is, rather, that *sum* is necessarily true whenever it is *considered*— that it is logically impossible for *sum* to be so much as formulated or entertained without being true. A proposition may be formulated in words ("uttered") or it may be formulated merely in thought

---

[8] *Principles of Philosophy*, Part I, sec. vii; HR I, 221; AT VIII, 7, ll. 4-7. Italics mine.

("conceived by my mind"). Descartes's point is that *sum* cannot be formulated at all unless it is true and that it is true, accordingly, whenever it is considered.

There is a third statement from which Descartes's conclusion must be distinguished. When he asserts that *sum* cannot be considered without being true, Descartes is not claiming that whoever considers *sum* inevitably believes it—that *sum* is indubitable in the sense that it can never be doubted by anyone. Descartes does hold that there are some propositions incapable of being considered without being believed, but *sum* is not among those characterized in this way. Here are two relevant passages:

> *Of those* [*things that are perceived clearly by the intellect*] *some are so evident and at the same time so simple that we never think of them without believing that they are true—e.g., that I, while I am thinking, exist; that things that are once done cannot be undone; and the like. . . . For we cannot be in doubt about them unless we think about them, but we cannot think about them without at the same time believing that they are true. . . . Therefore we cannot be in doubt about them without at the same time believing that they are true—i.e., we cannot ever be in doubt* [*about them*].[9]

> *When, however, we apprehend that it cannot happen that something comes from nothing, then the proposition* ex nihilo nihil fit *. . . is called a general notion or an axiom. Countless others are of this kind: "It is impossible that the same thing should both be and not be," "what is done cannot be undone," "he who thinks cannot not exist while he is thinking." Indeed all* [*such propositions*] *. . . must be acknowledged when the occasion occurs for us to think about them and when we are not blinded by prejudices.*[10]

The characteristic with which Descartes is concerned in these passages is not the one that he ascribes to *sum* in (*d*). In (*d*) he says that *sum* cannot be considered without being true, while in the passages just quoted he speaks of what cannot be considered without being believed.

It is apparent that what Descartes has in mind in the quoted

---

[9] HR II, 42; AT VII, 145, l. 22—146, l. 4.
[10] *Principles of Philosophy*, Part I, sec. xlix; HR I, 238-239; AT VIII, 23, l. 24 — 24, l. 6.

passages are logically necessary statements. His inclusion of "I, while I am thinking, exist" among these statements confirms, incidentally, that he regards the connection between his thinking and his existing as simply a case of an elementary logical entailment. The passages do not refer to *sum* at all. The propositions to which they refer do not affirm existence but merely relate it to thinking: "I, while I am thinking, exist" and "He who thinks cannot not exist while he is thinking." In (*d*), on the other hand, a categorical statement is at issue: "I exist."

It is clearly one thing for a proposition to be true and another thing altogether for its truth to be apparent to someone who is considering it. What Descartes says about *sum* in (*d*) is far from being tantamount to the claim that *sum* is known to be true by whoever considers it. So far as (*d*) goes, it is quite possible for *sum* to be considered without being believed and, a fortiori, without being known to be true.

This does not make it any more difficult to understand Descartes's conclusion in (*d*) as being that *sum* is in an important sense indubitable. Although (*d*) does not assert that *sum* is indubitable in the descriptive sense of the term—according to which what is indubitable is what cannot in fact be doubted by anyone—there are other senses of indubitability as well. In particular there are normative senses, according to which what is indubitable is what there is no reason to doubt or what there can be no reason to doubt. Descartes's intention in (*d*) is, as a matter of fact, to assert that *sum* is indubitable in a normative sense. I shall now attempt to explicate this sense of indubitability.

When Descartes opens his discussion with a question about *sum* he is not actually proposing an inquiry about a single statement but about the members of an indefinitely large class of statements. There is a temporal reference implicit in *sum*—"I exist *now*"— which differs on each occasion that *sum* is asserted or considered. Now it is not his existence at any particular time that Descartes is concerned about. In setting out to test the belief that he exists against the doubts generated in the First Meditation, it is not any particular statement—"I exist at time t_1"—whose indubitability preoccupies him.

Indeed it is quite obvious that no such statement can be altogether immune to doubt. There is some time at which a person can readily doubt his own existence at any given time; there is always some time t_2 at which a person may reasonably doubt his own existence at time t_1, where t_2 differs from t_1. The question that interests Descartes is whether there can be a time at which he could not reasonably count on his own existence *at that time*. He wants to know whether there could ever be an occasion when it would be reasonable for him to refuse assent to the statement "I exist now." Why this question interests him will be considered later.

The peculiar certainty of *sum*, which Descartes seeks to establish, may be elucidated by contrasting it with the indubitability of various other types of statement. There are many logically contingent statements which, when they are true, may be known with certainty. Statements about the sensory content of experience, for instance, are widely supposed to be of this sort. Thus a person who feels a pain may reasonably regard his belief that a pain is occurring as entirely beyond his doubt. But suppose that a person does not feel pain. Then it may be quite reasonable for him to doubt that a pain is occurring; he can be certain, moreover, that he himself is feeling no pain. The statement that a pain is occurring may be beyond a person's doubt on some occasions but dubitable on others. And a person's statement that he himself feels pain is one that he may at certain times properly regard as indubitable, while at other times he may know quite well that it is false.

The situation is similar with regard to empirical statements. Although a person may sometimes have for an empirical statement evidence that leaves no room for doubt, it may be reasonable for him to doubt the statement at other times when this evidence is not available to him. Moreover, if the statement were in fact false, it might be quite possible for him to have conclusive evidence of its falsity or at least to have evidence sufficient to justify a reasonable doubt concerning its truth.

Finally, there are statements that are rendered true by the mere act of making them, such as "I am making a statement." Because of their self-confirming character, statements of this sort cannot be made falsely. Nonetheless there are occasions when they can reasonably be doubted or when they can be known to be false. When I am not making a statement, I may know that I am not. There may be circumstances in which I am simply not sure whether what I am doing constitutes making a statement, and in those circumstances I can reasonably doubt whether I am doing so. The same holds, of course, for more straightforward and commonplace performatives, such as "I hereby promise to do such and such." When I am not promising, I may be well aware that I am not; and in certain circumstances I may have a reasonable doubt as to whether what I am doing really constitutes the making of a promise.

Statements of the sorts just considered may be beyond doubt under certain conditions, but there are also conditions under which they may reasonably be doubted or known to be false. Everything depends upon the evidence that is currently available or upon what is currently happening. A person can never, on the other hand, have good reason to doubt his own existence. As Descartes says in (*d*), it is logically impossible for there to be an occasion on which a person considers the statement *sum* and on which the statement is false. The indubitability of *sum* thereby differs from the indubitability that a statement may enjoy at certain times and not at others.

Sum is not altogether unique in this respect. There are many statements concerning which it is contradictory to suppose that someone considers them while they are false or that someone believes them falsely. All logically necessary truths have this characteristic. Although logically necessary statements resemble *sum* in this, however, they differ from it in other important ways. For one thing, they are entirely formal in content and involve no assertion of existence; *sum*, on the other hand, is a synthetic and logically contingent statement in which the existence of something is asserted. This renders it of greater relevance to Descartes's inquiry.

There is another difference as well, closely related to the first. Although it is contradictory to suppose that a person entertains or believes either *sum* or a logically necessary statement while it is false, the source of the contradiction is not the same in the two cases. In the latter case it is due to the fact that the denial of a logically necessary statement is self-contradictory. This means that recognizing the indubitability of such a statement involves recognizing that the statement is true. In the case of *sum*, however, the situation is otherwise. When Descartes recognizes that there is a contradiction in supposing that he entertains or believes *sum* while it is false, this is by no means tantamount to his knowing that *sum* is true.

For the indubitability of *sum* is not a function of its logical status or of its truth, but of its relation to the supposition that it is entertained or believed. Thus the conclusion that Descartes draws in (*d*) does not entail his existence, nor does he need to know that *sum* is true in order to be able to affirm the conclusion. This becomes fully apparent if the point made in (*d*) is applied to some person other than himself. Descartes's conclusion is quite general in import and readily permits such applications. It justifies, for instance, the following assertion: "It is necessarily the case that the statement *I exist* is true whenever Caesar pronounces or conceives it." Someone who recognizes that this assertion is correct clearly does not thereby commit himself to regarding *Caesar exists* as true.

Descartes's discussion is not devoted to proving that *sum* is true in the sense of deriving it validly from securely established premisses. It is easy to be misled about this, for a variety of reasons. The discussion begins, after all, with what is apparently a question about the truth of *sum*. Immediately following the end of his discussion, moreover, Descartes says: "But I do not yet sufficiently understand *what* I am, I who already necessarily am." (The approved French translation is more lucid: "I do not yet know clearly enough what I am, I who am certain that I am.") This suggests strongly that he regards *sum* as having been proven. Finally, it is apparent that Descartes is concerned with establishing that *sum* is indubitable, and it is very natural to suppose that this must be tantamount to a concern with proving that *sum* is true. Against these considerations, however, is the plain fact that the final conclusion of Descartes's discussion in (*d*) involves no commitment to the truth of *sum*, as well as the fact that *sum* is never categorically asserted in the course of his discussion. These facts bear on the question of what Descartes is interested in asserting, though not of course on the question of what he is entitled to assert.

It seems to me that Descartes is no more interested in the fact that he exists than he is in the facts that he considers in the First Meditation, for instance, that he is seated by a fire, wearing a dressing gown, and so on. Even if he had started out by taking these facts for granted, instead of by suspending judgment about them, the course of his inquiry would hardly have been affected. For his fundamental concern is not with the empirical question of what the facts are but with the epistemological and metaphysical question of how to attain certainty. His primary interest in the various facts he discusses is not in whether or not they are truly facts, but in whether it is reasonable for him to be entirely certain of them. When he considers the belief in his own existence, similarly, his aim is not to establish its truth-value but to reveal its indubitability. His conclusion does, to be sure, justify an assertion of *sum*. But the justification does not consist in a proof of *sum*. It consists in a proof that *sum* can never reasonably be doubted.

Descartes tries to show that *sum* is indubitable in the sense that he never runs any risk in believing it. His point is not that he has or that he could have conclusive grounds for asserting *sum;* that point, as I have observed, could be made correctly about numerous statements. What he seeks to establish is that whenever he raises the question of his existence—that is, whenever he considers *sum* —it must *always* be reasonable for him to assert that he exists; he need *never* be in doubt about his existence.

Now why is it this particular sort of indubitability that Descartes finds so essential to his enterprise? An important clue to the answer can be found in the opening sentence of the First Meditation, where he announces that his intention is to build anew "from the first foundations" in order to establish something *"solid and permanent* in the sciences" (my italics). Scientific beliefs cannot be relied upon to be solid and permanent if there is any chance that their foundations will turn out to need revision. As he proceeds to develop a system of science, accordingly, Descartes requires a foundation that *can never* be subject to doubt. He must have statements for which reasonable grounds for doubt are logically impossible. Otherwise he will always be troubled by a lingering concern that such grounds will one day be discovered and that the structure the statements support will totter in consequence.

But this in itself does not account for his refusal to settle for anything less than the kind of indubitability that characterizes *sum.* When a person has a pain he can be quite certain of the belief that he has one, without fear that subsequent evidence will require him to reject it or to hold it in doubt. Why is such a belief unsuitable to serve as a foundation for science? The reason is that a person cannot always be certain that he has a pain, for sometimes he does not have one. The certainty of beliefs concerning the content of consciousness is, as it were, contingent upon the occurrence of those contents. But the certainty of *sum* is not contingent in this way, since a person can never be aware that he does not exist.

The certainty of *sum* is, so to speak, ubiquitous and inescapable; it has a kind of generality. Because of its generality or inescapability, *sum* may be regarded as a kind of necessary statement despite the fact that it is logically contingent; it may not be improper, indeed, to regard it as a synthetic necessary statement. The certainty that may be enjoyed by statements of other sorts, on the other hand, lacks this characteristic. Their certainty may not be available when it is needed since, unlike *sum*, these statements are detachable from the facts that confirm them. *Sum* is entailed by the mere fact that it is being considered—it is not detachable from what confirms it. The certainty of *sum* is always current. There can never be an occasion when a person need admit doubts concerning it.

I will mention another point, although its relevance is a matter for speculation. Descartes is working toward the establishment of a foundation for scientific thinking, and there is an obvious advantage in providing a foundation that is sharable or transferable from one scientific thinker to another. If the foundation consisted of statements about the content of consciousness, it would differ from one scientist to the next; for one man's experience is not that of another. If it consists of statements like *sum*, however, each scientist can begin from a similar point. Everyone can be certain of his own existence, but different men can be certain only of the different contents of their own particular consciousnesses. Descartes never says anything to show that he has this point in mind, however, which is why I say that its relevance is speculative.

One of Descartes's doctrines may at first sight seem very difficult to reconcile with what he says about *sum* in the Second Meditation. This is the doctrine that no one can be really certain of anything until he knows that God exists. Since Descartes does not arrive at a knowledge of God's existence until the Third Meditation, how can he properly regard *sum* as indubitable in the Second? In his Reply to the Second Objections, he indicates how this difficulty is to be resolved. There he explains:

> *When I said that* we can know nothing with certainty unless we first recognize that God exists, *I declared in plain terms that I was speaking only of the knowledge of conclusions* the memory of which can recur when we are no longer attending to the arguments on the basis of which we deduced them.[11]

No one can proceed very far in science if he must keep before his mind at all times the evidence for the various statements already established that provide the basis upon which he seeks to develop additional knowledge. He must be able to rely upon his conclusions in the past without having to be constantly aware of the proofs that guarantee them. But if he is not aware of their proofs, how can he be confident that the statements he has previously established are acceptable? He must obviously count on the recollection that the statements were once satisfactorily proven.

Now Descartes's contention is that this recollection is not suffi-

[11] HR II, 38; AT VII, 140, ll. 12-16. My emphasis.

cient; no one can be really certain of a statement he remembers having once proven unless he knows that God exists. As Descartes makes clear in the passage just quoted, however, it is not necessary to know that God exists in order to be certain of a statement for which one has conclusive evidence immediately before him.

The need for God's guarantee arises only with regard to statements that are detachable from what confirms them. If there can be an occasion on which a statement may be considered without conclusive grounds for it being available, then there can be an occasion on which the statement may reasonably be doubted unless God's existence is known. But *sum* is not a statement of this kind. It is not detachable from evidence that confirms it. A conclusive ground for it is currently available whenever it is considered, since the ground consists simply in the fact that it is being considered. This ubiquity or generality of *sum*'s certainty accounts for the fact that Descartes reaches the conclusion of his discussion of his existence without making a categorical affirmation of *sum*. The purpose of his discussion is to show that he can count on *sum* whenever he needs it, rather than to affirm it as a current truth.

Descartes's reply to Gassendi about *ambulo ergo sum* is somewhat misleading, for it tends to obscure the character of the indubitability that *sum* enjoys. One point upon which the case for this indubitability rests is that Descartes's existence is entailed by his considering *sum*. This entailment is taken entirely for granted in the discussion. Descartes never analyzes it and never subjects it to doubt; he treats it as palpably self-evident and unexceptionable. It is a "clear perception of the intellect"—that is, a logical truth. Like other logical truths, such as "what is once done cannot be undone," it is "so evident and at the same time so simple" that it cannot be doubted.

But it is also a logical truth that *sum* follows from *ambulo*. The fact that his existence is entailed by his walking is no less evident to Descartes than that it is entailed by his thinking. Each entailment is an equally clear-cut instance of "B(a) entails $(\exists x)(x = a)$." Descartes would be unable to accept *sum* as indubitable, however, if he knew only that it is entailed by *ambulo*. For the question of whether *sum* is true can arise when *ambulo* is not true, and on such an occasion he would have no ground for affirming his existence.

The critical point here is not that *ambulo* is a physical object statement and therefore one that the skeptical arguments of the First Meditation render uncertain. Even if Descartes could be certain about whether or not he is walking, the realization that his existence is entailed by his walking would still not enable him to regard *sum* as indubitable in the relevant sense. For it might be false that he is walking on some occasion when he considers his own existence, and then, if he knew only that *sum* is entailed by *ambulo*, it would be reasonable for him to doubt his existence.

In his reply to Gassendi, Descartes locates the essential difference between *cogito ergo sum* and *ambulo ergo sum* in the "metaphysical certitude" of *cogito*. This suggests that the advantage of deriving *sum* from *cogito* rather than from *ambulo* lies in the fact that *cogito* is immune to the doubts still besetting statements about the physical world, such as *ambulo*. Descartes explains, indeed, that the reason he regards *ambulo ergo sum* as unsatisfactory is that "the motion of the body sometimes is non-existent in dreams, when nevertheless it seems to me that I am walking."[12] Thus he describes the superiority of *cogito ergo sum* as due to the fact that he can be certain of *cogito*, whereas the dream argument undermines the certainty of *ambulo*.

It seems, however, that Descartes misrepresents his own case here. The relevant difference between *cogito* and *ambulo* is not, as he says, that he can be certain of the former but not of the latter; it is that the former is inseparable from *sum* whereas the latter is not. If the account of the matter that he gives to Gassendi were actually correct, there would be a serious gap in Descartes's discussion of his existence in the Second Meditation. For nowhere in that discussion does he either show or assert that *cogito* (or any similar statement) escapes the doubts raised in the First Meditation against statements concerning physical things. If the peculiar value of deriving *sum* from *cogito* actually consisted in the certitude of *cogito*, Descartes ought to establish or at least to claim that *cogito* is in fact a statement of which he can be certain. He does not do so.

The most plausible place to look for an argument establishing the premiss from which *sum* can be inferred is in the third step of his discussion, but the certainty of such a premiss is not considered there at all. In (*c*), Descartes first remarks that his existence is entailed by his being deceived; then he asserts that he cannot be deceived about his existence when he thinks that he exists. It is not relevant that he might have argued, had he chosen, that he cannot be deceived about whether or not he is thinking. The fact is that he

[12] HR II, 207; AT VII, 352, ll. 13-15.

presents no such argument. He concerns himself in (*c*) only with showing that the demon's powers of deception cannot subvert his belief that he exists. Neither in this step nor elsewhere in his discussion does he make the point that *cogito* (or any similar statement) cannot be doubted.

Despite what he says to Gassendi, the indubitability of *cogito* is not part of the case Descartes makes in the Second Meditation for the indubitability of *sum*. The latter does not depend on his ability to maintain a premiss like *cogito* even in the face of the possibilities that he is dreaming or that there is a demon out to deceive him. His discussion of his existence in the Second Meditation is not devoted to showing that he can *prove* that he exists by first becoming certain that he is thinking and then deducing his existence from this premiss. Instead of showing that *sum* can be deduced from a premiss that is certain in its own right, Descartes in effect points out that a premiss from which *sum* can be elicited is an essential and inescapable element of every context in which the need for assurance concerning *sum* arises. The permanent availability of *sum* rests upon its derivability from a premiss that is necessarily available whenever it is needed.

A puzzling feature of Descartes's inquiry is the variety of premisses from which he asserts that his existence is inferable. In (*b*) the premiss is that he *thought of something*. In (*c*) he says that he exists whenever he *believes that he exists*. In (*d*) he commits himself to the claim that he exists whenever he so much as *considers the belief that he exists*. Elsewhere in his writings, moreover, he speaks of inferring his existence from the premiss that he is doubting something.[13] What accounts for this variation?

Each of the inferences is, of course, equally legitimate. But they are not equally appropriate to Descartes's final purpose in his discussion. The most general of them is *cogito*, since it is entailed by all the others; doubting, being deceived, thinking that one exists, considering the belief that one exists—these are all cases of *thinking*. None of the other premisses, then, has the same degree of ubiquity as *cogito*, since none of them is in turn entailed by it.

The premiss to which Descartes refers in the final step of his discussion, however, has a degree of ubiquity that is cut to the measure of his need. There are times when a person can realize that he is neither doubting his existence nor thinking that he exists, and

---

[13] *The Search After Truth*, HR I, 324; AT X, 523. Cf. also *Principles of Philosophy*, Part I, sec. vii; HR I, 221; AT VIII, 6-7.

at such times *sum* cannot be derived from these premisses. But while there may well be times when a person is not considering his own existence, it is clear that he is *ipso facto* doing so whenever he becomes interested in the question of whether he is entitled to assert *sum*. Moreover, a person can never be aware that he is neither uttering *sum* nor conceiving it in his mind: to be aware of this would necessarily involve formulating *sum*, either in words or in thought, and would accordingly not be an awareness that *sum* was not being formulated. Even without claiming that he can be certain of whether he is thinking or of whether he is considering *sum*, therefore, Descartes can properly maintain that a premiss entailing *sum* can never be lacking on an occasion when the reasonableness of asserting *sum* becomes a question.

It is clearly important for Descartes to establish that *sum* is certain, but doing so does not solve the fundamental epistemological problem he raised in the First Meditation. That problem was not to identify propositions more worthy of unreserved assent than the sensory beliefs in which his confidence had been undermined. It was to discover a rule of evidence more reliable than the rules of sensory evidence that his skeptical arguments discredited. Descartes does not propose a solution to this problem until the Third Meditation, when he formulates his principle of clear and distinct perception: "It seems to me that I can establish as a general rule that everything I perceive very clearly and distinctly is true."[1]

What is "clear" and "distinct" perception? Descartes offers some useful explanations in *Principles of Philosophy,* a book in which he presents his doctrines in the synthetic mode.[2] But he provides no very explicit or deliberate definitions of these terms in the *Meditations;* he introduces them there more or less informally, almost as though they were not technical terms at all. Presumably, since the *Meditations* is written in the analytic mode, he believes that readers who carefully reconstruct the development of his views can gather the meanings of the terms for themselves. It is appropriate, therefore, to try to elucidate his notion of clear and distinct perception by considering how, in the *Meditations,* he derives the first knowledge that he characterizes as being clear and distinct.

Some commentators, particularly those who base their interpretation of Descartes's philosophy largely on the *Discourse on Method*, suppose that he elicits the principle of clarity and distinctness by reflecting on the paradigmatic certainty of *sum*. Copleston, for example, gives the following account of the matter:

[1] HR I, 158; AT VII, 35, ll. 13-15.
[2] *Principles* I, xlv, xlvi; HR I, 237; AT VIII, 21-22.

> *By examining a proposition which is recognized to be true and certain, he hopes to find a general criterion of certainty. And he comes to the conclusion that there is nothing in the proposition, I think, therefore I am, which assures him of its truth except that he sees very clearly and distinctly what is affirmed.*[3]

Now this is quite accurate as far as what Descartes says in the *Discourse* is concerned, but it does not fit the procedure that he follows in the *Meditations*.

In both the *Discourse* and the *Meditations*, as a matter of fact, Descartes postpones introducing the principle of clarity and distinctness until he has gone beyond discovering that his existence is certain and has reached a conclusion concerning his nature. This in itself suggests that he may not think it possible to derive the principle simply from his initial certainty that he exists. In the *Meditations* (though not in the *Discourse*), moreover, he indicates rather clearly that reaching a conclusion beyond the belief that *sum* is certain is of decisive relevance in his derivation of the principle:

> *I am certain that I am a thinking thing. Do I not then know also what is required in order that I be certain of something? Surely there is nothing in this first cognition except a clear and distinct perception of that which I affirm; and that, indeed, would not suffice to render me certain of the truth of a thing if it could ever happen that something I perceive so clearly and distinctly should be false. Accordingly it seems to me that I can establish as a general rule that everything I perceive very clearly and distinctly is true.*[4]

Descartes does not, in this passage, identify the "first cognition" that leads him to the principle of clarity and distinctness as having to do merely with the fact that he exists. He identifies it as the knowledge that "I am a thinking thing." Not just *sum*, but *sum res cogitans*.

If there are discrepancies in the various accounts Descartes gives of this matter they are due less, I believe, to lapses in consistency or changes in opinions during the course of his philosophical career, than to the very close relationship he conceives to hold between the statement that he is a thinking thing, and the statement *sum* as it occurs in his proof that his existence is certain. I shall endeavor to show that in the *Meditations* he initially presents the statement that he is a thinking thing as nothing more than an explicit rendering

---

[3] Frederick Copleston, *A History of Philosophy*, Vol. IV (Garden City: Doubleday, 1963), p. 97.

[4] HR I, 158; AT VII, 35, ll. 6-15.

of *sum.* If I am correct in this, it is natural enough that he should sometimes be inclined to treat the two statements as more or less interchangeable.

Immediately after he reaches the conclusion that *sum* is certain, Descartes recognizes that his knowledge of himself is not sufficiently clear and, in order to clarify it, sets out to distinguish himself from other things. He proposes to find a more distinct conception of the "I" and, in so doing, to perceive more clearly what he is:

> *But I do not yet know clearly enough what I am, I who am certain that I am. I must continually beware lest I imprudently take something else in place of myself and thus go astray even in that very cognition that I contend is the most certain and most evident of all.*[5]

Descartes devotes two consecutive passages, following these remarks, to the task of attaining a clearer and more distinct perception of his own nature:

Passage A

> *What then did I formerly suppose myself to be? A man, of course. But what is a man? Should I say a rational animal? No, for then I should have to ask what an animal is, and what it is to be rational, and thus I should slide from one question into many that are more difficult. . . . I should rather attend here to the spontaneous thoughts to which nature previously led me whenever I considered what I am. Surely it occurred to me first of all that I have a face, hands, arms, and that whole mechanism of members (just as one observes in a cadaver) which I designated by the name of body. It occurred to me besides that I am nourished, that I walk, that I have sensations, and that I think, which actions I attributed to the soul. But what the soul is, either I did not consider or else I imagined it to be a very subtle sort of thing —on the model of wind, or fire, or the ether, which is infused throughout the grosser parts of me. . . .*
>
> *But what now, when I suppose that a most powerful and, if one may say so, malicious deceiver bent every effort to deceive me in all things as much as he could? Can I affirm that I have even the least of all those things that . . . pertain to the nature of body? I consider, I think, I turn it over in my mind—I hit upon no such thing. I grow weary of going over the same things in vain. But what of those things that I attributed to the soul—being nour-*

---

[5] HR I, 150; AT VII, 25, ll. 15-18. The first sentence of this translation follows the French rather than the Latin text.

ished or walking? But since I have no body these too are nothing but fictions. Having sensations? Surely this also occurs only with a body, and I have seemed to sense many things in dreams that I later observed I had not sensed. Thinking? Here I find it! It is thought! This alone cannot be stripped from me. I am, I exist; that is certain. But when? Surely as often as I think; for it might even be the case that if I were to stop thinking entirely I should likewise altogether cease to be. I am now admitting only what is necessarily true; all that I can say, therefore, is that I am a thinking thing—that is, a mind, or spirit, or intellect, or reason —words whose signification was formerly unknown to me. I am, however, a real, a truly existing thing. But what sort of thing? As I have said: a thinking thing.[6]

Passage B

And what else? I shall exercise my imagination. I am not that collection of members called the human body. Nor am I a subtle air infused through those members—not wind, not fire, not a vapor, not a breath—not anything that I picture to myself; for I have supposed that such things are nothing at all. This supposition remains in force. Nevertheless I am something. But perhaps these very things that I am supposing to be nothing (since they are unknown to me) are nevertheless really no different from what I know as myself. I do not know. I am not disputing this matter now; I can pass judgment only regarding things that are known to me. I have come to know that I exist; I ask what I am —I whom I have come to know. It is most certain that the knowledge [of my existence] considered precisely does not depend on things whose existence I have not yet come to know. Therefore it does not depend on any of those things that I picture in my imagination. . . . But I already know for certain that I am and, at the same time, that all these images (and in general whatever pertains to the nature of body) may be nothing but dreams. . . . And so I know that those things that I can comprehend with the help of the imagination in no way pertain to the knowledge I have of myself, and that the mind must most diligently be called away from them so that it may perceive its own nature most distinctly.

But what then am I? A thinking thing.[7]

It is very frequently supposed that in these passages Descartes

[6] HR I, 150-152; AT VII, 25-26, l. 10; 26, l. 24—27, l. 16.
[7] HR I, 152-153; AT VII, 27, l. 17—28, l. 8; 28, ll. 15-20.

attains what he regards as a clear and distinct perception that his essence is to think. Each of the passages ends, after all, with the assertion *sum res cogitans*, which sounds as though it is intended to be a formulation of his essence. In the corresponding passage of the *Discourse on Method*, moreover, he affirms that he is "a substance the whole essence or nature of which is to think."[8] It is quite natural, then, to interpret the two long passages just quoted as developing Descartes's familiar doctrine that he is essentially a thinking thing. But this interpretation involves, despite its plausibility, insurmountable difficulties. Anyone who accepts it will be bound to find an egregious inconsistency in Passage A and another unmistakable inconsistency in Passage B. If Descartes really does claim in these passages that he is essentially a thinking thing, his discussion of the matter is severely flawed in a most unlikely way.

The two inconsistencies are clearly visible on the very surface of Descartes's text. In Passage A he says that thought alone "cannot be stripped from me." But shortly after he makes this statement, in which he seems to assert that thought is essential to him and that he cannot exist without it, he observes: "it might even be the case that if I were to stop thinking entirely I should likewise altogether cease to be." Now if he regards thought as one of his essential properties, much less as his only essential property, how is it possible to account for this "might be"? Given the belief that thought is essential to him, he has no ground whatever for hesitation; he should understand that ceasing to think *would* mean ceasing to exist. Conceding that he might exist even without thinking seems blatantly inconsistent with his affirmation that thought is the one thing of which he cannot be deprived.

The inconsistency in Passage B is similar. In that passage Descartes first categorically denies that anything bodily is essential to him, then acknowledges that bodily things may be identical with him after all. He appears to say, in other words, both that nothing bodily is included in his essence, and that something bodily may actually be essential to him.

One way to resolve these inconsistencies, without giving up the idea that Descartes is concerned in the two passages with defining his essence, is by invoking his metaphysical doubt concerning the reliability of clear and distinct perception. This line of argument would be that when he admits in Passage A that he might exist without thinking, and when he admits in Passage B that bodily

[8] HR I, 101; AT VI, 33, ll. 4-5.

things may not be different from himself, he bases his admissions solely on the radical possibility that even what is clearly and distinctly perceived may be false. He acknowledges that thought may not really be his only essential characteristic, even though he perceives clearly and distinctly that it is, because he is not yet altogether convinced that what is clearly and distinctly perceived is true. He does perceive clearly and distinctly that thought is his essence, according to this account, but he hedges the claim because he still fears the demon.

This is an appealingly convenient way of dealing with the conflict between what Descartes says in Passages A and B and the initially plausible view that he intends in these passages to identify thought as his essential characteristic. But it simply will not do. A decisive consideration against it is that the two passages occur before he has so much as formulated the principle of clarity and distinctness, and thus before it can even have occurred to him that the principle may be unreliable. It is altogether illegitimate to invoke his subsequent doubts concerning clarity and distinctness in order to explain what he says before these doubts have arisen in the course of his inquiry.

If Descartes were already troubled by metaphysical doubts concerning clear and distinct perception, he should also have reservations later in the Second Meditation about his thesis that the essence of a piece of wax is to be extended, flexible, and movable. Regarding clear and distinct perception as the basis of his view of the nature of the wax is at least as reasonable as regarding it as the basis of his belief that he is a thinking thing. And if the metaphysical doubt is invoked against the one, it should also be invoked against the other. But Descartes does not hedge his assertion about the wax in the same way that he hedges his assertion about himself. This tends to confirm my claim that the metaphysical doubt is not at work in his discussion of his nature.

There is only one other way to deal with the inconsistencies in Passages A and B, and that is to give up construing these passages as involving a definition of his essence. It is difficult in any case to believe that Descartes ever regarded himself as essentially nothing but a thinking thing. The doctrine that thought is the essence of *mind* is rather plausible, perhaps, but does Descartes think that he is essentially nothing but a mind? When he raises the question of what his nature is, his first answer is that he is a *man*. He puts aside the definition of man as a reasonable animal, because it leads to too many further questions, but does not discard the statement that he is a man. This statement is a correct answer, he believes, to the question of what he is. He continues throughout his work to regard it as correct, and continues to think that in order to understand his nature he must discover what it is to be a man. Now it is quite implausible to suggest that to be a man is essentially just to be a thinking thing. In the Sixth Meditation Descartes formulates a conception of himself as a union of body and soul. This is surely his conception of what it is to be a man and of what he essentially is.

The intent of his discussion of his nature in the Second Meditation is not entirely clear. One of his concerns in the *Meditations* is to establish the possibility that the soul is immortal, and it is therefore important for him to show that there is a real distinction between body and soul. Descartes sometimes gives the impression that he thinks he has established this distinction in Passages A and B, but whether or not he has, the statement that body and soul can exist separately is by no means equivalent to the statement that a man is essentially nothing but a soul or a thinking thing. Descartes's essence is to be a man, and men are surely not immortal, even if their souls may be. In the light of these considerations, of course, it is rather inaccurate to say that Descartes establishes the certainty of his own existence in the Second Meditation. What he establishes is the certainty of his existence insofar as he is a thinking thing. Not until the Sixth Meditation is he in a position to establish his existence as a man.

His conclusion in the Second Meditation that he is a thinking thing means only that thought is the one characteristic he can justifiably ascribe to himself at the current stage of his inquiry. The import of his discussion in Passages A and B is, in fact, simply to clarify what he has already established in his examination of *sum*. He does not, in the two passages, define the essence of the object whose existence he has shown to be indubitable. He only identifies that object by making explicit the characteristic through which he has come to know it.

Descartes's discussion of *sum* is not complete when he reaches the conclusion that "I exist" is certain, for the meaning of the term "I" is not very clear to him. Even after he has developed a proof that *sum* is certain, he does not fully understand exactly what the proof proves. He still understands the "I" in *sum* as little more than "something"; for him to make any use of the certainty with which his proof provides him is therefore dangerous. The danger is that

119

he may erroneously identify the object of whose existence he is certain; he may mistakenly slip into regarding as indubitable the existence of some other object—an object whose existence is not rendered certain by his arguments concerning *sum*.

Although Descartes's initial understanding of himself is merely that he is a "something," the argument by means of which he shows that *sum* is certain provides him with resources permitting him to infuse additional meaning into his conception of the "I." His knowledge of himself is not just the knowledge of some unidentifiable "x"; it is the knowledge of an object whose existence is rendered indubitable by the considerations he has marshaled in establishing that *sum* is certain. Despite the fact that he has not yet advanced beyond thinking of himself as a "something," therefore, a richer conception of the "I" is implicit in his discussion of *sum*. He can complete his examination of the belief that he exists by attaining a more explicit appreciation of just what it is that his discussion of *sum* shows to be immune to doubt.

The discussion that results in his affirmation of *sum res cogitans* gives content to the "I" in *sum*. The only question that Passages A and B answer, then, is this: *What character may Descartes properly ascribe to himself on the basis of the way in which he has shown that he cannot doubt his own existence?* When he has answered this question he has made explicit the conception of the "I" that is implicit in his conclusion that *sum* is certain. He has at least partially identified the object whose existence he has shown to be indubitable. Accomplishing this does not settle the question of whether the characteristic by which he has come to know himself is essential to his existence, nor does it exclude the possibility that other characteristics are essential to it. His identification of himself as a thinking being neither asserts nor entails either that thought is essential to his existence or that no property other than thought is essential to him. It merely expresses what, at the stage of his inquiry described in the Second Meditation, he is entitled to believe about the "I."

Let me explain how, in the light of this interpretation, certain critical sections of Passages A and B are to be understood. In the first passage Descartes says:

> *Thinking? Here I find it! It is thought! This alone cannot be stripped from me. I am, I exist; that is certain. But when? Surely as often as I think; for it might even be the case that if I were to stop thinking entirely I should likewise altogether cease to be. I*

am now admitting only what is necessarily true; all that I can say,
therefore, is that I am a thinking thing.

When he speaks here of what is "necessarily true," Descartes is not
referring to logically necessary statements. The statements he has
in mind are those that must be true—i.e., those that follow logically
—*given* what he already knows. It is necessary in this sense that
they be true, but they need not themselves be necessary truths.

Now what Descartes already knows is that his existence is rendered indubitable by what I shall call "the *cogito* argument"—the
considerations that establish the certainty of *sum*. Taking the
meaning of "I" *precisely* means including in its meaning all and
only the characteristics necessarily belonging to an object whose
existence can be shown to be certain by the *cogito* argument. Descartes defines the precise meaning of "I" as it appears in the conclusion of that argument, accordingly, when he formulates a characterization of himself logically equivalent to the statement that the
argument renders his existence certain. After he has determined
that what goes into this characterization is just that he is a thinking
thing, he is not entitled to offer *sum res cogitans* as a logically
necessary statement or as a definition of the essence of the object
denoted by the "I" in *sum*. For all he knows, that object may have
essential characteristics to which the *cogito* argument provides no
clue; the argument may seize the object by a merely incidental
handle, so to speak, which does not enable him to grasp the real
nature of the object considered in itself. Descartes propounds *sum
res cogitans*, therefore, only as a description of himself and not as
a definition of his essence. Although it defines "I" as the term
appears in the conclusion of the *cogito* argument, it does not define
the essence of the object denoted by "I." (Suppose I have evidence
that my wife recently obtained something for twenty-three dollars.
Then I can infer the existence of something for which she paid that
amount, but I surely cannot infer that its essence is that it cost her
twenty-three dollars. I may observe, moreover, that when I established the existence of something my wife purchased I did not
assume that there are any shoes in the world. Does this mean that
what my wife purchased was not a pair of shoes?)

If Descartes is not defining his essence when he asserts that he
is a thinking thing, what is to be made of his statement that thought
is the *only* thing of which he cannot be deprived? To say that no
property but one is indispensable to the existence of something
leaves open, to be sure, that some disjunction of other properties

121

may be indispensable; the essence of some object might be to have property P and either property Q or property R. Descartes's statement is not quite tantamount, therefore, to the assertion that thought alone constitutes his essence. But he says that thought is indispensable to his existence, and this surely suggests that he regards it as at least belonging to his essence.

This suggestion can be avoided by taking into acount the context in which Descartes makes the statement in question. He has been considering various physical characteristics involved in his common-sense conception of himself, and has observed that the demon hypothesis, although it precludes his ascribing any of these characteristics to himself, does not interfere with his belief that he thinks. Thought, then, is the only characteristic that he can confidently ascribe to himself *on the basis of what he now knows or believes*— namely, that his existence is certain, that there is a demon, and that there is no physical world. This does not mean that thought is his only essential characteristic, however, or even that he cannot actually exist without thinking. If *sum* is to be taken precisely, it must be understood as referring only to a being that thinks; this is the meaning of "I" as it figures in the conclusion of the *cogito* argument. Hence Descartes limits his idea of himself to the conception of a thinking being. At this point, however, he is not equipped to consider whether this conception adequately construes the real nature of the being whose indubitable existence he has established.

He knows himself, as it were, only under a certain description: "the object whose existence is shown to be indubitable by the *cogito* argument." But he may be knowable under other descriptions as well, and some of these may lead to a conception of what is essential to him that includes characteristics other than thinking. The demon hypothesis, for all he now knows, may be false; it may even, for all he now knows, turn out to be self-contradictory. In that case he may eventually find out that there really are (or even that there must be) physical things, and he may discover either that his own existence is not possible without some of these things or that some of them are sufficient for his existence. Thus the "might be." Descartes supposes that there are no bodily things, and therefore the conception of himself that figures in the conclusion of the *cogito* argument cannot be a conception of something bodily. But this means only that he does not now understand the term "I" to refer to something with bodily characteristics. It does not follow that he himself has no such characteristics, nor does it follow that no bodily characteristics are essential to his existence. He is simply not yet in a position to consider these matters effectively. "I do not know," he says in Passage B; "I am not disputing this matter now; I can pass judgment only regarding things that are known to me."

Each of the two passages A and B makes explicit one feature of the conception of himself that is implicit in Descartes's *cogito* argument. In the course of that argument, the fact that he is thinking suffices to show him that he exists. Now what may be inferred from this concerning the meaning of the "I"? What must be the character of a thing whose existence is established by the fact that it is thinking? At the very least, obviously, it must be a thing that thinks. Descartes's conception of himself includes, accordingly, the idea that he is a thinking thing. Does it include anything else? This is the subject of Passage B, which begins with the question "And what else?" The only other candidates for inclusion that Descartes considers are of a physical sort: bodily parts and processes. None of these can belong to the conception of the "I" in the *cogito* argument, however, since Descartes establishes the certainty of his existence in that argument while continuing to deny that anything physical exists. The conception of himself that is implicit in the *cogito* argument, accordingly, is a conception of a thinking thing and only of a thinking thing. In the statements in which he seems to fall into inconsistencies, Descartes is actually making a special point of disclaiming any intention to decide whether the characterization of himself implicit in the *cogito* argument grasps any or all of what is essential to his existence.

As a result of the discussion conducted in Passages A and B, Descartes says, "I begin to know what I am a little more clearly and distinctly than before." In just what does this increase in clarity and distinctness consist? Descartes achieves it by arranging a precise coincidence between what he ascribes to himself and the character that he recognizes as necessarily belonging to an object whose existence can be rendered indubitable by the *cogito* argument. I suggest, then, that perceiving something clearly and distinctly is a matter of recognizing that it is "necessarily true." On the basis of what I have already said, however, it is apparent that what is clearly and distinctly perceived need not be a necessary truth in the sense that its denial is self-contradictory, but only necessarily true in the epistemic sense that no coherent grounds for denying it are consistent with the perceiver's basis for believing it. A basis for belief may be another belief, as when someone infers a conclusion from a premiss that he knows to be true; or it may be some experience, as when a person bases his belief that there is a table in the room on the fact that he sees a table there. When a person perceives something clearly and distinctly, his basis for believing it is so complete that no additional evidence could strengthen it. Since there is nothing further that he must consider, there is no reasonable basis for him to withhold assent or to doubt. His clear and distinct perception consists in the recognition that this is the case.

A clear and distinct perception involves on the one hand a certain logical relationship between what is being perceived and the perceiver's basis for believing it, and on the other the apprehension or perception that this relationship obtains. It is important to recognize that clarity and distinctness are not properties of the objects of perception. The point of Descartes's doctrine is not that there is a class of clear and distinct objects, whose clarity and distinctness are perceptible to any reasonable person who examines them carefully. Given two equally reasonable and attentive men, one may perceive something clearly and distinctly while the other does not; and the same person may have a clear and distinct perception of something on one occasion but not on another, even though he is equally reasonable and perceptive at the two times. This is so because whether it is consistent for a person to deny something may depend upon what else he is aware of or knows, and two people (or the same person at different times) may be aware of or may know different things. The fact that one person perceives clearly and distinctly that he is in pain in no way suggests that this must be clearly and distinctly perceived by everyone else. The availability to someone of a clear and distinct perception depends upon his own actual epistemic situation and not simply upon abstract logical considerations.

Descartes's rule of clarity and distinctness is actually little but a more explicit formulation of the criterion for belief recommended in the opening sentence of the First Meditation, where he insists upon beliefs that will be "solid and permanent." He is dissatisfied with the instability of opinions that are accepted merely because they are plausible or probable; he demands unshakable beliefs that can therefore serve appropriately as foundations for science. He requires, in other words, beliefs to which he can commit himself without any risk whatever that he will some day need to revise or abandon them.

When a person bases his acceptance of a belief on a clear and

distinct perception, he recognizes that he cannot consistently conceive reasonable grounds for doubting the belief. The falsity of the
belief is incompatible with his basis for believing it; given that basis
it is logically impossible that the belief should turn out to be false.
Since he cannot intelligibly foresee any circumstances that would
show the belief to be false, a person is justified in regarding the
belief as unshakably solid and permanent. The first of the four rules
of method that Descartes presents in the *Discourse* expresses the
matter as follows:

> *The first of these [rules] was to accept nothing as true which
> I did not clearly recognize to be so: that is to say, carefully to
> avoid precipitation and prejudice and to include in my judgments
> nothing more than what was presented to my mind so clearly and
> so distinctly that I could have no occasion to doubt it.*[9]

Perceiving something clearly and distinctly involves having a basis
for believing it that is logically complete. To settle for a basis
weaker than this is to be too hasty or precipitous in judgment, or
to prejudge the case before the basis for judgment is adequate to
support a judgment in which unqualified confidence can reasonably
be placed.

The rule of clarity and distinctness has a somewhat different
status than the other rules of method formulated by Descartes in
the *Discourse* and elsewhere. Unlike the others, it is not so much
a rule of method as a criterion of evidence. Indeed, Descartes's
other methodological precepts are essentially rules of procedure for
arriving at clear and distinct perceptions. A familiar complaint
against his theory of knowledge is that he fails to explain how to
distinguish such perceptions from others. But his method is precisely a method for reaching clear and distinct perceptions; the
distinction between them and others is just the distinction between
perceptions that can be attained by a conscientious and correct use
of the method and those that cannot be thus attained.

The most that can be said for any method is that its precepts are
intelligible and practicable, and that it will lead to the desired result
if correctly used. Whether or not Descartes's method is practicable
may be disputed, but it cannot be disputed that he does provide a
method designed to discriminate between perceptions that are clear
and distinct and those that are not. The complaint that he provides
no criterion for identifying clear and distinct perceptions is therefore a rather curious one, in view of the extent to which he develops

[9] HR I, 92; AT VI, 18, ll. 16-23.

and advertises a method for doing just that.

The principle of clear and distinct perception will be considered more exactly and in greater detail in the next chapter. I wish now to complete my discussion of *sum res cogitans* by differentiating the roles of Passages A and B and by dispelling, insofar as I am able to do so, the somewhat puzzling impression of redundancy that the two passages give. This appearance of redundancy is actually rather striking. For one thing, the second passage ends with the very same conclusion—*sum res cogitans*—that is enunciated at the close of the first. For another, Descartes sometimes seems to ignore in the second passage what the first has already accomplished. Thus he says near the beginning of Passage B: "Nevertheless I am something." Now he did, to be sure, establish this assertion by the *cogito* argument. But he also established, in Passage A, a stronger assertion: "I am a thinking thing." Why does he ignore the fact that he has just asserted *sum res cogitans* and revert or regress to the vaguer statement "I am something," beyond which his inquiry has already advanced?

It is reasonable to suppose, even without an explicit statement to that effect in the *Meditations*, that the *distinctness* of a perception has to do with the perceiver's ability to *distinguish* what he perceives from what he does not. This suggests that Descartes arrives at a distinct perception of himself as a thinking thing in Passage B, where he decides that his conception of himself *excludes* everything physical. In Passage A, on the other hand, he considers what is *included* in this conception: he examines various possibilities and then finds that thought cannot be "stripped" from him. In other words, it becomes *clear* to him that he thinks. In Passage A, then, Descartes reaches a clear perception that he is a thinking being. Once he sees clearly that he is a thinking being he is anxious to "pass judgment *only* regarding things that are known" to him. His concern in Passage B, accordingly, is to distinguish what is clear to him from other things and to ensure that his judgment covers no more than what is clear to him. In the second passage he defines the limit of his judgment and thereby arrives at a distinct perception that he is a thinking being.

A trace of redundancy remains, however, even after it is recognized that Passage A establishes a clear perception that *sum res cogitans* and that Passage B renders the perception distinct. This is due partly to the fact that questions concerning what is clear and questions concerning what is distinct tend to merge. Reaching a distinct perception is actually a matter of getting clear about precisely what is being perceived; it consists in recognizing what is clear and what is not clear. The remaining trace of redundancy also has its source partly in the procedure that Descartes follows in Passage A: he selects what is clear to him from among the various candidates considered, and in rejecting all but thought he tacitly affirms that being a thinking thing is the only thing that is clear to him. That is why Passage B, which makes this point openly, seems a bit supererogatory. The apparent redundancy of the two passages would have been diminished if Descartes had not begun by reviewing and rejecting a number of candidates for inclusion in his conception of the "I," but had merely said straight out that he is aware of thinking. Presumably he chooses not to proceed in this way because he wishes to emphasize a point that he expects his readers to find difficult and implausible: the point that the existence of thought is more accessible to knowledge than the existence of anything physical.

127

12 CLEAR AND DISTINCT PERCEPTION

A convenient way to begin developing a more detailed understanding of Descartes's rule of evidence—that is, his rule of clarity and distinctness—is to consider what sorts of objects he supposes to be clearly and distinctly perceived. This aspect of his doctrine is frequently misunderstood, which sometimes results in making the theory of clear and distinct perception appear quite outrageously foolish. Fairly good sense can be made of the theory, I believe, if care is taken to avoid certain more or less enticing errors of interpretation.

When Descartes introduces his rule in the Third Meditation, what he says indicates that he has propositions in mind as the objects of clear and distinct perception. He refers to the perception of *what I assert;* and what one asserts, it is plausible to say, is a proposition. He gives as his paradigm the perception *that I am a thinking thing;* and this is how propositions are generally denoted. The rule itself, moreover, ascribes truth to whatever is clearly and distinctly perceived; and it is propositions that have truth-values. At various other places in his writings, however, Descartes gives the impression that non-propositional objects may be clearly and distinctly perceived. He frequently speaks of his clear and distinct ideas of God and of matter, for example, and his language on these occasions suggests that he has in mind the perception of objects more naturally thought of as concepts than as propositions.

One way to interpret the variation in Descartes's usage would be to suppose that he believes some perceptions have propositions, while others have concepts, as their objects. Is this in fact his view? There are some obvious difficulties in supposing it is. Concepts are *con*ceived, one is inclined to say, not *per*ceived. The notion of perceiving a proposition is fairly intelligible: it is simply a matter of perceiving *that such-and-such is the case.* But what is it to perceive a concept?

These difficulties might be circumvented, without doing any great violence to what Descartes says, by revising his rule of evidence so that it asserts that whatever is clearly and distinctly perceived *or* conceived is true. But then another difficulty would be confronted. Concepts are not the sorts of things, it would seem, that can be true or false. A concept may be logically coherent, or well-defined, but in what sense can it be assigned a truth-value? Now this question is actually rather easy to deal with in terms of Descartes's views; he himself provides, indeed, a clear basis for the answer. Even if the objects of clear and distinct perception must be entities with truth-values, it is quite consistent with his views that the class of these objects should include both concepts and propositions.

Descartes makes a distinction between "formal" and "material" truth-values, such that neither concepts nor propositions have truth-values in the formal sense:

> *For although I have pointed out that it is only in judgments that falsity, properly so-called, or formal falsity, can be found, still there surely is another kind of falsity in ideas—material falsity—when they represent what is not a thing as if it were a thing. . . . And . . . there can be no ideas that do not appear to be ideas of things.*[1]

Only judgments, according to Descartes's usage, are in the strict, or formal, sense true or false. Now what is clearly and distinctly perceived is certainly never a judgment. Judgments may, of course, be based upon or justified by clear and distinct perceptions, but judgments are made, not perceived. If the object of perception is true or false, therefore, it can only have a truth-value in the material sense. Since it is not a judgment, it can have no formal truth-value. But it is just as easy to assign material truth-values to concepts as it is to assign them to propositions. The proposition that Paris is in France is materially true if it represents something actual, i.e., if Paris is actually in France. By the same token, the concept of a winged horse is materially true or false depending upon whether it represents something or nothing, i.e., whether or not there are any winged horses.

The problem of whether it is propositions or concepts that are clearly and distinctly perceived is not solved, then, by insisting on the condition that the objects of perception must have truth-values.

[1] HR I, 164; AT VII, 43, ll. 26-30; 44, ll. 3-4.

This condition is satisfied in the same sense both by propositions and concepts, so that it does not serve to eliminate the possibility that the latter as well as the former may be objects of perception. For all that I have so far said, accordingly, either a proposition or a concept may be clearly and distinctly perceived. The fact that the objects of perception must be true or false does not entail that concepts are not among these objects.

There are good reasons, nonetheless, for rejecting the view that Descartes's rule of evidence applies both to propositions and concepts. His language at times does suggest this view, and neither of the difficulties just discussed is very troublesome. But these difficulties are only the most uninteresting ones prompted by this interpretation. Much more serious is the fact that if Descartes's rule of evidence is construed to refer to concepts as well as propositions, then it is natural to ascribe to him an extremely peculiar and unlikely theory of truth. For if clear and distinct concepts are materially true, then the existence of an object is inferable from the fact that a person has a clear and distinct conception of it. Descartes would be saddled, if this were actually his view, with the grotesque doctrine that all questions of existence can be decided by conceptual activity alone. It would be his belief that a person need only formulate a clear and distinct idea of some type of object in order to be certain that an object of that type exists.

According to this interpretation, then, Descartes is committed to an apriorism far more radical than St. Anselm's. Anselm believed that the existence of God can be established merely by considering the idea of God, but Descartes is made out to believe that the existence of *any* sort of thing can be established simply by constructing a clear and distinct concept of it. Now Descartes surely does not believe this. In the Second Meditation he reaches a clear and distinct conception of matter as something extended, flexible, and movable. But he does not conclude from his possession of this concept that there are material things; on the contrary, he continues to doubt that there are any such things.

What he *does* think himself entitled to infer in this case is only that all material things are actually extended, flexible, and movable; and this is consistent with the nonexistence of any matter at all. Descartes has a clear and distinct concept of matter as having certain essential properties, and the conclusion that his rule of clarity and distinctness justifies is simply that these properties do necessarily characterize every material thing. The point is that having a clear and distinct concept is not, for Descartes, an altogether non-propositional affair. It is not exclusively a matter of formulating or entertaining a well-defined idea of a certain configuration of properties and relations, but of perceiving that the concept in question necessarily involves certain properties or relations.

To have a clear and distinct concept of something is to perceive what characteristics necessarily belong to it. The doctrine that a clearly and distinctly conceived concept is true means only that the concept does actually include the properties and relations perceived to be implicit in it, and that anything that fits the concept necessarily has those properties and relations. It does not mean that some object corresponding to the concept must exist. Even when Descartes seems to identify the object of a clear and distinct perception as a concept, accordingly, what he perceives is something propositional. He does not simply have the concept in the sense of entertaining it in his mind. He perceives *that* the concept necessarily involves certain properties or relations.

In this light the question of whether concepts as well as propositions may be objects of clear and distinct perception appears less pointed. A clear and distinct perception is always a perception *that something is the case.* It always has a proposition as its object. But the proposition may be about what is necessarily involved in some concept; it may be a proposition about a concept. In such cases Descartes sometimes says that he has a clear and distinct idea, or a clear and distinct concept, instead of saying that he clearly and distinctly perceives a proposition.

The widespread misunderstanding of the nature of clear and distinct perception may be traced in part, I believe, to an analogy Descartes sometimes invokes between the sort of perception referred to in his rule of evidence and ordinary vision. This analogy tends to suggest that the perception of a proposition is a kind of direct confrontation involving simply a proposition on the one hand and a perceiver on the other. The perception is often understood (e.g., by Kemp Smith[2]) as a variety of immediate experience in which something is *given*, not to one of the senses but to the understanding.

Starting with this picture, and wondering how to understand successful (i.e., clear and distinct) perception in terms of it, it is easy to suppose that a clear and distinct perception can only be a con-

---

[2] Norman Kemp Smith, *New Studies in the Philosophy of Descartes* (London: Macmillan & Co., 1963), pp. 55-56.

frontation in which the intrinsic nature of the perceived proposition is fully apparent to the perceiver. After all, if nothing goes into the perceptual situation but a perceiver, a proposition, and the perceiver's "vision" of the proposition, how can better and worse perception be differentiated except in terms of whether what the perceiver is aware of is or is not conformable to the nature of the object? As for the question of what it is to be aware of the nature of a proposition, the most natural answer is that it consists in understanding the proposition's meaning. In this way, then, the analogy with vision leads to the notion that perceiving a proposition clearly and distinctly is essentially a matter of having a lucid and thorough understanding of it.

Now perceiving a proposition clearly and distinctly does, of course, involve understanding it and paying careful attention to its meaning. There must be more to clear and distinct perception than this, however, if Descartes's ascription of truth to what is clearly and distinctly perceived is to make any sense. It would certainly be an error to foist upon him the extraordinary claim that the truth of a proposition may be inferred from the fact that someone understands it. Moreover, while clear and distinct perception does involve a direct apprehension of something by the understanding, it is not correct to construe the perception simply as a matter of an immediate experience. To do so is to reduce Descartes's doctrine to a crudely implausible psychological theory of truth, and to ignore the essentially logical import of his conception of evidence.

Another source of confusion about Descartes's rule of clear and distinct perception is the fact that he often characterizes what is perceived as an "idea." Now one view of ideas is that they are entirely constituted by the apprehension of them: an idea is simply whatever is apprehended by the person who has it. An idea is a *given*, in other words, and it has no being or nature apart from what is given. Descartes frequently seems to endorse this view. Ideas, he says, are "all that which is in our mind when we conceive a thing"[3]; our awareness of them is "immediate."[4] But if an idea is simply whatever is immediately apprehended, every idea is exactly what it appears to be, and then there is no basis for making a distinction between ideas perceived clearly and distinctly and those perceived less satisfactorily. If an idea is nothing but what someone is aware of, it seems that every awareness of an idea must be perfect. For

[3] AT III, 392-393; letter to Mersenne, July 1641.
[4] HR II, 52; AT VII, 160, 1. 15.

the idea has no character other than what is apprehended, and it is identifiable only as what is given to awareness.[5]

These difficulties can be resolved once it is recognized that the situation in which clear and distinct perception occurs includes more than just a perceiver and a proposition or an idea. Consider how Descartes develops his first clear and distinct perception. As he begins the inquiry that leads to *sum res cogitans,* he already has a rudimentary or incipient "idea" of himself as something whose existence is shown to be certain by the *cogito* argument. He wishes to learn what *this* idea does and does not include. The content of the idea that he is exploring is *fixed,* so to speak, by the following specification: it involves all and only those properties that must belong to something whose existence is rendered indubitable by the *cogito* argument. Were it not for this specification, which fixes the meaning of "I," Descartes would have nothing to go on. He could, of course, consider any number of conceptions or statements about his nature; he could explicate each of them and distinguish it from the others. But he could then do no more than contemplate them indifferently, for he would have no criterion for deciding which among them actually gives the meaning of "I" that he is seeking.

Descartes's problem after the *cogito* argument is not just to formulate some proposition concerning his nature and to understand what that proposition means. His problem is to elicit *the* meaning of "I" that has been fixed in his earlier discussion of *sum;* or, what comes to the same thing, to understand precisely what proposition concerning his nature is conclusively justified by the considerations marshaled in the *cogito* argument. That argument provides him, in effect, with a description of the concept in which he is interested —"the concept of an object whose existence is rendered certain by such-and-such considerations"—and the task he sets himself is to develop an explicit account of the conception that fits this description. His search for a clear and distinct idea is an analytical enterprise, therefore, which involves more than a mere attentive confrontation of something given to awareness.

Perceiving something clearly and distinctly is essentially a matter of perceiving certain logical relationships. These relationships are not exclusively within the object perceived; they do not all hold between parts of the object, as does the relationship between the subject and predicate of a proposition or between the various con-

[5] Cf. Alan Gewirth, "Clearness and Distinctness in Descartes," *Philosophy,* XVIII (1943).

stituents of a concept. Hence perceiving them is not tantamount simply to understanding the logical structure or the meaning of the object. Some of the relevant relationships hold, except in the cases of certain necessary statements, between the proposition perceived and an evidential basis for believing it that is provided either by another proposition or by some experience.

Descartes thinks there are a number of very elementary propositions that need only be understood in order for it to be apparent that they cannot reasonably be doubted.[6] These propositions are self-evident in the sense that they are clearly and distinctly perceived, and thus known to be true, whenever their meanings are attentively grasped. But it is a mistake to construe his theory of clear and distinct perception as a theory of self-evidence. Even the clear and distinct perception of a self-evident proposition involves more than apprehending the proposition itself; it requires recognizing that no possible state of affairs is inconsistent with the proposition. And in all other cases of clear and distinct perception the evidential basis for the proposition perceived is external to it; it is quite possible that the proposition should be thoroughly understood without being perceived clearly and distinctly. In the Second Meditation Descartes begins with the proposition that *sum* is rendered certain by the *cogito* argument and goes on to determine that, given this proposition, it is inconceivable that *sum res cogitans* is false. But it is equally possible to start with a proposition whose truth-value is unknown and then to seek a clear and distinct perception of it by finding an evidential basis that excludes all reasonable grounds for doubting it. Whatever the order, the logical situation is the same.

The mere perception of this logical relation between a proposition and something that is considered as an evidential basis for it is not, of course, equivalent to a clear and distinct perception of the proposition. A person does not perceive clearly and distinctly that something is the case merely by recognizing that its falsity cannot be conceived when something else is given. The "something else" —the basis—must itself be beyond reproach. It is obvious that not all clear and distinct perceptions can have as their bases propositions that have been clearly and distinctly perceived. The bases for some clear and distinct perceptions are provided by the "self-evident" propositions to which I have already referred. The bases for others are provided by experiences, such as a feeling of pain or the occurrence of a certain thought.

[6] HR II, 42; AT VII, 146.

When a person considers a proposition in connection with something that he thinks may provide a satisfactory (i.e., logically conclusive) evidential basis for it, I will say that a "perceptual situation" occurs. There are many perceptual situations, of course, in which nothing is clearly and distinctly perceived. Grounds for doubting the proposition being considered in a certain situation may be conceivable even given the evidential basis in question. Even if they are not conceivable, moreover, the person involved in the situation may fail to perceive that they are not; thus he may miss a clear and distinct perception that he is actually in a position to have. Every perceptual situation does, to be sure, include materials for the clear and distinct perception of *something;* for some proposition is conclusively established by anything that can serve as an evidential basis. But a person may not think of any such proposition, or he may not see that its falsity is inconceivable given the basis for it that he has before him.

Clear and distinct perception is a matter of recognizing that there are no reasonable grounds on which a proposition can be doubted. But just what is clarity and what is distinctness? The relations between them are very close. Distinctness may be defined in terms of clarity, in fact, as Descartes himself suggests: "when something is clear [I call] it distinct if it is so divided and separated from everything else that it plainly contains nothing but what is clear."[7] Whatever is perceived distinctly, then, is also perceived clearly. A perception may be clear, on the other hand, without being distinct.

In *Principles of Philosophy,* Descartes gives the following illustration of these relationships:

> *While someone is feeling a great pain the perception of the pain is certainly very clear in him, but it is not always distinct. For men commonly confuse that perception with their obscure judgment as to its nature. They suppose that in the part giving them pain there is something similar to the sensation of pain, which is all that they perceive clearly. And so there can be a clear perception that is not distinct, but none that is distinct without being clear.*[8]

In the perceptual situation Descartes describes here, the evidential basis is a feeling of pain. Now a person who is feeling pain may have no interest in any proposition at all, and therefore he may have no clear perception that he is in pain. But a person who is feeling pain

[7] *Principles of Philosophy,* I, xlv; AT VIII, 22, ll. 6-9.
[8] *Principles of Philosophy,* I, xlvi; AT VIII, 22, ll. 10-17.

cannot coherently suppose that he is not doing so. It is *clear* to him, if he adopts a cognitive attitude toward the situation, that he is in pain. But he may mistakenly believe that his feeling also justifies some proposition concerning the source of the pain in his body. Descartes maintains that the feeling itself is not a conclusive guide to any such bodily source. Although a person in pain may perceive clearly that he is in pain, he does not thereby perceive clearly that his body is affected in any particular way.

If someone does not take care to distinguish precisely between what is and what is not conclusively justified by the evidential basis with which his pain provides him, he may readily mistake his perception that he is in pain for a perception that his body is affected. He may erroneously suppose, according to Descartes, that the occurrence of his pain excludes all reasonable grounds for doubting some proposition about his body. In that case he has not distinguished what is clear to him from what is not; his perception that he is in pain is clear, but not distinct. He perceives the proposition that he is in pain indistinctly if he supposes either that it is equivalent to the proposition that his body is affected or that it entails this proposition. Descartes's discussion of pain shows, incidentally, that there may be clear and distinct perceptions of propositions concerning sensory matters. There is nothing in the notion of clear and distinct perception to suggest that this should not be so. It is equally apparent, however, that clear and distinct perception cannot be accomplished by the senses. It is exclusively, Descartes insists, an activity of the understanding or reason.

The claim that clear and distinct perception is an affair of reason by no means commits Descartes to eschewing the use of the senses in inquiry. It means only that whether a person has a clear and distinct perception of some sensory matter depends upon how he interprets or understands the sensory data in question, and not simply upon his awareness of them. "Pain, color, and other things of that sort are clearly and distinctly perceived," Descartes says, "when they are considered just as sensations or thoughts."[9] An animal may have a pain but not a clear and distinct perception that he has it. The latter involves measuring the sensory datum against a proposition; it requires an intellectual activity, which only a rational creature can perform.

It may seem difficult to understand the sort of situation in which a person perceives a proposition clearly without also perceiving it

[9] *Principles of Philosophy*, I, lxviii; AT VIII, 33, ll. 10-12.

distinctly. Suppose that a man understands pain, as Descartes does, to be entirely a psychic phenomenon with no necessary connections to any bodily event; and suppose that the man feels a pain and considers the proposition that he is in pain. In that case, according to Descartes, his perception of the proposition will be both clear and distinct. But suppose, on the other hand, that the man regards pain as including a bodily as well as a psychic dimension. In that case he seems to be considering a different proposition altogether —one in which there is a quite different concept of pain than the concept involved in the first case. Since this second proposition requires the existence of his body, it would seem that he perceives it *neither* clearly *nor* distinctly. How, then, can his perception that he is in pain be clear but not distinct?

This difficulty is serious only if it is assumed that no proposition can be considered at all without its meaning being thoroughly understood, or that the same proposition cannot be taken to have different entailments. No doubt there is a close relationship between the meaning of a proposition and what the proposition entails, and considering a proposition does surely presuppose some understanding of what it means. If understanding it is identified with knowing what it entails, however, absurdities quickly develop. For this means that a person can never be mistaken about what a proposition entails, since he cannot consider the proposition at all without knowing what it entails. And it also follows that two people who disagree about what a proposition entails cannot be thinking of the same proposition and therefore cannot actually be disagreeing.

In fact it is precisely in errors of this sort about what a proposition entails—in this lack of clarity—that the indistinctness of a perception consists. A proposition is clearly perceived when the perceiver recognizes that his evidential basis for it excludes all reasonable grounds for doubting it. A perception is distinct, on the other hand, when the perceiver understands what is and what is not entailed by the evidential basis that renders his perception clear. To perceive distinctly that one is in pain, accordingly, is to understand this proposition as including all and only what is entailed by the feeling of pain constituting the evidential basis for it. Then the perception includes, as Descartes says, nothing except what is clear.

It may be useful to relate this discussion to Descartes's development in the Second Meditation of his paradigm of clear and distinct perception. The result of the *cogito* argument is his clear perception that *sum* is indubitable. This perception is not distinct, however, until he goes on to discriminate between what his argument does and does not establish. His position at the end of the *cogito* argument is similar to that of a man suffering pain who perceives clearly that he has a pain, but who is not sure whether or not this is tantamount to perceiving clearly that some part of his body is affected. Just as the sufferer whose perception is not distinct may tend to suppose that he has a clear perception that his body is affected, so Descartes may slip into thinking that he has a clear perception that the existence of a physical thing—a human body—is indubitable. Just as the sufferer may improperly identify his pain with some state of his body, so Descartes may imprudently take some other object in place of himself.

Descartes's problem, at the end of the *cogito* argument, is to see to it that his perception that *sum* is certain includes nothing but what is clear to him. Now when he determines that the conception of the "I" in *sum* is a conception of something that thinks, he perceives that his evidential basis for the perception that *sum* is certain conclusively establishes that the existence of a thinking thing is certain. He perceives clearly that he—understanding himself to be the object whose existence is rendered indubitable by the *cogito* argument—is a thinking thing. This perception makes the perception that *sum* is certain somewhat more distinct, since it serves to distinguish *sum* from propositions that do not concern thinking things. Taking this step, then, accomplishes two things. It gives Descartes a clear perception of himself as a thinking thing, and renders his perception that *sum* is certain more distinct than it was before.

When he determines further that the conception of the "I" in *sum* is not a conception of a thing with physical characteristics, Descartes recognizes that the evidential basis supporting the proposition that *sum* is certain does *not* enable him to perceive clearly that the existence of something with physical properties is indubitable. Taking this step also accomplishes two things. It makes Descartes's clear perception of himself as a thinking thing more distinct. And it also increases the distinctness of his perception that *sum* is certain, by distinguishing *sum* from all propositions concerning the existence of physical things.

Descartes increases the distinctness of his perception that *sum* is certain, therefore, first by providing a clear conception of the "I" that figures in *sum* and then by providing a distinct conception of it. The statement *sum res cogitans* is no more than a clarified version of the *sum*, or "I am something," with which the conclusion of the *cogito* argument is concerned. Instead of perceiving merely that he is something, Descartes now perceives clearly that he is a thinking thing. His perception of this is distinct as well, since he realizes that perceiving *sum res cogitans* is not equivalent to perceiving that he is a thing with any physical properties. It is precisely because his perception that *sum* is certain is initially clear but *not* distinct that Descartes postpones introducing the principle of clarity and distinctness until after he has established *sum res cogitans.* For it is only when he arrives at this proposition that his perception becomes distinct as well as clear.

Increasing the distinctness of a clear perception does not in any way add to the evidence for the proposition that is perceived. No evidence can be stronger than that which constitutes the basis for a clear perception. But it is possible to recognize that something is certain without understanding exactly what it is that is certain, as in the case of Descartes's initial perception concerning *sum,* and in the case of someone who perceives clearly but indistinctly that he is in pain. Reaching a distinct perception, then, is essentially a matter of defining what is and is not clear. Now for any clearly perceived proposition, there are an unlimited number of other propositions not entailed by it or by its evidential basis. It is impossible, therefore, to render a clear perception entirely distinct by identifying each of the propositions included, and each not included, in it. How, then, can a person ever be in a position to decide that his perception includes nothing but what is clear? And if he can never actually arrive at this position, how much distinguishing must he do before he is entitled to decide that his perception is distinct enough?

Descartes often speaks of clear and distinct perception as admitting of degrees rather than as a matter of all or nothing. When he concludes the inquiry that leads him to *sum res cogitans,* for example, he says that he now begins to understand himself with *"a bit more* light and distinctness than before." There is also an obvious reference to the variability of clear and distinct perception in his formulation of his rule of evidence: "everything that I perceive *very* clearly and distinctly is true" (italics mine).

Passages such as these suggest that the clarity as well as the distinctness of a perception is susceptible of variations in degree. Now it is easy enough to understand the source of variations in distinctness: it lies in the extent to which what is clearly perceived is distinguished from what is not clearly perceived. But the account of clear perception that I have given precludes the possibility of any variations in clarity at all. Something is clear to someone, according to this account, when he recognizes that he has no coherent grounds for doubting it or when he understands that he cannot conceive its falsity. How can there be room in this conception for a distinction between greater and lesser clarity, any more than there is room for a distinction between greater and lesser degrees of validity among arguments?

Descartes is not very consistent in what he says about the degrees of clarity and distinctness. On some occasions his claim that one thing is clearer and more distinct than another means only that it is in a certain sense easier to know. At the end of the Second Meditation, for instance, he remarks:

> But if the perception of the wax has seemed more distinct after it has become known to me not by sight and touch alone but by many causes, it must be acknowledged that I am now much more distinctly known by myself, since there are no grounds that can aid the perception of the wax, or of any other body that do not, all of them, provide better evidence of the nature of my mind [emphasis mine].

When he says here that his knowledge of himself is superior in clarity and distinctness to his knowledge of the wax, Descartes means that the former is prior to the latter in the following sense: whatever provides him with knowledge of the wax also provides him with knowledge of himself, but not *vice versa*. In a way, therefore, a clear and distinct perception of himself is more accessible than a clear and distinct perception of the wax. But this has little to do with the notion I have been explicating of degrees of clarity and distinctness.

Descartes employs the term "clear" in two rather different senses. I have already explained one of these. The other is indicated by his observation that "no concept is called obscure or confused except because it contains something that is unknown."[10] Whatever can be logically demonstrated to belong to something with certain properties, according to Descartes, is "contained" in the concept of the thing; for example, whatever properties must belong to a three-sided plane figure are contained in the concept of such a figure. Distinctions in the degree to which a concept is clear to

[10] HR II, 43; AT VII, 147, ll. 9-11.

someone may thus be made on the basis of how much he knows of what the concept contains. If a person has a concept of a triangle as a three-sided plane figure but does not understand that the interior angles of a figure of this sort must equal 180 degrees, then he is ignorant of something that his concept contains and the concept is not entirely clear to him. It is easy to formulate an analogous notion of degrees of clarity in terms of propositions instead of concepts. In the same way that the concept of something with certain properties also includes whatever other properties such a thing must have, a proposition "contains" whatever it entails.

In one sense, then, a perception is clear when the perceiver recognizes that he has conclusive ξ ιunds for the proposition he perceives. There can be no degrees of clarity in this sense of the term. In another sense, however, something is clear to a person when it contains nothing of which he is ignorant. The basis for degrees of clarity in this sense is readily apparent. Clarity in the first sense has to do with a person's appreciation of the state of his evidence for some proposition. In the second, it refers to the extent to which he understands what the proposition involves. There is, as a matter of fact, a similar ambiguity in the ordinary non-philosophical usage of the term "clear." A person may say that it is clear to him that such-and-such is the case, meaning he has no doubts about it. And a person may also say that a proposition is clear to him, meaning he understands it and what it involves, without suggesting that he has any basis whatever for believing the proposition to be true. There is generally no great difficulty in understanding which of these senses of "clear" is intended in any specific context, and one can easily follow Descartes's uses of the term. Though his usage is not consistent his inconsistency does not reflect any significant philosophical or conceptual confusion on his part.

A concept or a proposition may, of course, contain a great deal that is not thought of by a person who enunciates it and who to some extent grasps its meaning. Descartes uses the term "adequate knowledge" to refer to the highest possible degree of clarity: "in order for any knowledge to be adequate," he says, "absolutely all the properties that are in the known thing must be contained in it."[11] This definition is formulated in terms of concepts, but an analogous definition in terms of propositions is easy to provide: adequate knowledge of a proposition embraces all that the proposi-

---

[11] HR II, 97; AT VII, 220, ll. 8-10.

tion entails. These definitions seem fairly straightforward; but there is some difficulty in understanding them, because Descartes gives apparently conflicting accounts of whether or not a finite mind can ever have adequate knowledge of anything.

He sometimes says that adequate knowledge is easy to come by. In the passage above from which his definition of adequacy is quoted, he explains to Arnauld that "in order to have adequate knowledge of anything, it is necessary merely to have . . . a power of knowing what is adequate for that thing, and this can easily occur." Presumably he means that when, for example, someone conceives a triangle as a three-sided plane figure, his conception is rich enough to enable him to derive all (or at least any) of the other essential properties of triangles. His knowledge of triangularity "embraces," in this sense, all the properties of triangles. If he thinks of triangles simply as plane figures, on the other hand, his knowledge of triangularity is not adequate; for many properties of triangles are not deducible from the fact that triangles are plane figures.

At other times, however, Descartes evidently understands "adequate knowledge" as requiring not just a power to derive all the properties necessary for the existence of a thing, but an *explicit* grasp of all these properties. In the *Conversation with Burman*, he comments as follows on his remarks to Arnauld concerning adequate knowledge:

> Let us take a triangle, for example—apparently a very simple thing—one of which we seem able easily to acquire adequate knowledge. Nevertheless we cannot acquire adequate knowledge of it. For even if we were to demonstrate all the attributes we can conceive in it, still, after a thousand years or so, another mathematician will detect more properties in it; and so we are never certain that we have comprehended all that could be comprehended about that thing. And the same can also be said of body and its extension and all other things. For there is no thing of which the author [i.e., Descartes] attributes to himself adequate knowledge, and yet he is certain that in respect of many things, if not of all, he has the sort of knowledge and foundations [for knowledge] from which adequate knowledge can be deduced and perhaps has been deduced. Who knows?[12]

In a similar vein he says to Gassendi: "you do not distinguish an act of the intellect in conformity with the scale of our intelligence

[12] Charles Adam, ed., *Entretien avec Burman* (Paris: Boivin, 1937), pp. 21-23; AT V, 151-152.

. . . from an adequate concept of things such as no one has . . . perhaps not even of anything, as small as you like."[13] The view that adequate knowledge requires merely the power to know whatever is included in a concept or proposition, and that it is therefore easy to come by, seems to me less authentically Cartesian than the view that adequate knowledge is difficult and perhaps impossible for humans to attain. In fact, Descartes sometimes uses a different term —"complete knowledge"—as a synonym for "adequate knowledge" in the weaker of these two senses.[14]

Even if someone should know everything that is contained in some proposition or concept, whether or not he would be able to realize that he did so is another question. Although Descartes gives two different accounts of whether it is possible to *have* adequate knowledge, he is quite consistent in maintaining that no man can ever *know* that he has it. Even in his reply to Arnauld, where he asserts that adequate knowledge is easy to come by, he denies that anyone except God can know that he has it. For "in order for him to know that he has that [adequate cognition of a thing], or that God has put nothing more in the thing than what he cognizes, his power of cognizing would have to be adequate to God's infinite capacity, which would obviously be absurd."[15] Since it is impossible to be certain that everything that is logically derivable from a concept or a proposition has actually been derived, no one can ever be altogether confident that his knowledge is adequate.

But this means that no man can ever know that he has an altogether clear and distinct perception, for in order to know this he would have to know that his knowledge is adequate. If something is obscure or confused when it contains something of which he is ignorant, and if he can never be certain that he is aware of everything a concept or proposition contains, then he can never be certain that his perception is altogether free of obscurity and confusion. Descartes apparently thinks that it is at the very least unlikely that any human knowledge is adequate, and he must therefore think that an entirely clear and distinct perception is equally unlikely. Now his rule of evidence says only that perceptions must be "very clear and distinct." Given that no perception is ever entirely clear and distinct, however, the question arises as to how clear and distinct a perception must be in order to satisfy his rule.

[13] HR II, 216; AT VII, 365, ll. 1-5.
[14] See HR II, 98, 220-221; AT VII, 221, 371.
[15] HR II, 98; AT VII, 220, ll. 17-21.

This question must be limited to one concerning the degree of *distinctness* that the rule requires. Descartes's view is surely that a proposition is to be accepted only if no reasonable grounds for doubting it are logically conceivable—only, in other words, if the proposition is perceived clearly in the sense in which clarity admits no variations of degree. The qualification "very" in his formulation of his rule of evidence must be discounted, therefore, insofar as it relates to the clarity of perception. This leaves the question of how distinct a perception must be if the proposition perceived is to be accepted confidently as true. Descartes does not answer this question, and it is actually impossible to give any very precise answer to it. No perception can be entirely indistinct; a person who is unable to distinguish a given proposition from *any* other does not understand it at all and can hardly be said to perceive it. To demand complete distinctness, on the other hand, is not reasonable; even if it is attainable a person cannot know that he has attained it. But between these two extremes no specific degree of distinctness can be identified as the ideal. The degree of distinctness that is appropriate in a particular case depends on the special circumstances of the case.

The only general rule is that each perception should be so distinct that the perceiver will not confuse what is clear to him with what is not. This rule is necessarily vague, because whether or not a person understands a proposition well enough to avoid confusion depends upon such a variety of circumstances that it is not plausible to try to give a fully codified account of them. In the case of his perception of *sum*, Descartes is concerned about the relation between this proposition and those having to do with physical things. He does not perceive the proposition distinctly enough, therefore, unless he understands this relation. There are any number of propositions, on the other hand, with which no one is likely to confuse *sum*. A person's perception of *sum* would not be defectively indistinct because he had not explicitly distinguished *sum* from all of these.

The question of the degree of distinctness necessary in order to satisfy Descartes's rule of evidence comes down to the question of how well a person needs to understand a proposition before he can reasonably make use of it in the conduct of philosophical or scientific inquiry. The sensible response is that this problem admits of no general solution; it calls for an exercise of judgment in each case. The appropriate degree of distinctness will always be a function of the uses to which the proposition in question is to be put, and of the confusions concerning it that seem likely to be troublesome. There is no alternative to being alert to these considerations and to making a decision in their light. The very fact that Descartes makes no attempt to define how much distinctness his rule requires suggests that he accepts this view.

It is difficult to see how anything much better than this general recommendation of prudence could be provided. After all, how distinctly *should* a person understand what he believes? Surely the only reasonable answer is that he ought to understand it distinctly enough to avoid making mistakes when he relies upon it. Everything will depend on what he is relying upon it for and on what sorts of mistakes he is likely to make. Perhaps a few maxims or rules of thumb might be useful. But the ability to recognize when a distinction is needed, and to recognize when making a distinction is nothing but mindless pedantry, is part of the intelligence and lucidity that no set of methodological precepts can effectively replace. The ability is itself essential, indeed, for the effective use of any set of rules. Even in the last analysis—*especially* in the last analysis— there can be no mechanical procedure for deciding when an appropriate degree of distinctness has been reached. The vagueness of Descartes's rule of evidence with respect to the prescribed degree of distinctness is inescapable, then, simply because there can be no exact general answer to the question of how to be intelligent.

13 OBJECTIONS TO DESCARTES'S RULE OF EVIDENCE

Descartes was aware of most of the points that critics of his principle of clarity and distinctness have made, and he attempted to forestall or correct the misunderstandings upon which many of them rest. The most widespread complaints against his rule allege either that the criteria it enunciates are too subjective, or that it is too vague to be used effectively. Descartes's theory of evidence does have certain limitations, but a great deal of the criticism leveled against it has been misguided.

C. S. Peirce raised several objections, finding, in the first place, that the rule is too restrictive:

> Descartes . . . maintained that if a man could only get a perfectly clear and distinct idea . . . then that idea must be true. But this is far too severe. For never yet has any man attained to an apprehension perfectly clear and distinct . . . and yet I suppose that true ideas have been entertained.[1]

Now I have argued in the preceding chapter that perfect clarity and distinctness are not required by Descartes's rule. Descartes does not, in any event, deny that many true propositions have been entertained without being clearly and distinctly perceived. His rule is not supposed to provide a unique and comprehensive criterion of truth, but only of evidence, and he does not pretend that there are no true propositions except those for which someone has satisfactory evidence. What he demands is just that no proposition should be accepted into the body of philosophical and scientific theory unless the evidence for it satisfies his rule of clarity and distinctness.

Peirce rejects this demand and, in doing so, concedes that using his own less stringent rule of evidence means abandoning Des-

---

[1] Charles Hartshorne and Paul Weiss, eds., *Collected Papers of Charles Sanders Peirce* (Cambridge, Mass.: Harvard University Press, 1935), 5.593.

cartes's ideal of unshakable belief. It is, of course, entirely fair for Peirce to raise the question of whether philosophy and science should admit beliefs that one could reasonably regard as corrigible. His fallibilism is an arguable alternative to Descartes's infallibilism. In some of his comments on Descartes's rule, however, Peirce attacks a palpably distorted version of the notion of clear and distinct perception. Thus, after remarking that "Cartesianism . . . teaches that the ultimate test of certainty is to be found in the individual consciousness," Peirce declares that Descartes's rule of evidence "amounts to this: 'Whatever I am clearly convinced of, is true.' "[2] And, in another passage, he develops the theme that Descartes's rule embodies a radically subjectivist criterion of truth:

> *Self-consciousness was to furnish us with our fundamental truths, and to decide what was agreeable to reason. But since, evidently, not all ideas are true, [Descartes] was led to note, as the first condition of infallibility, that they must be clear. The distinction between an idea* seeming *clear and really being so, never occurred to him.*[3]

Someone who knew nothing of Descartes's views but these characterizations of them would naturally suppose that the Cartesian criterion of evidence is of the most slovenly and irrationally willful sort.

Peirce suggests that clear and distinct perception is a matter of nothing more than how a person feels about a proposition, and that Descartes regards the bare fact of conviction as a reliable guide to truth. But Descartes's rule of evidence gives no weight at all to the mere fact that someone is convinced of something. What it prizes is not the absence of doubt, or even someone's inability to doubt, but the impossibility of finding reasonable grounds for doubt. This is a matter of logic, not of feelings, and is a long way from finding the marks of truth in states of consciousness.

Having a clear and distinct perception does not consist in feeling some sort of intellectual satisfaction that excludes all desire to doubt. Still less is it a matter of experiencing some esoteric luminescence exuded by true propositions. It is a rather straightforwardly logical matter of recognizing that no coherent grounds for doubting a proposition are conceivable, and of understanding the proposition well enough to avoid confusion. Given this interpretation of the doctrine, two points may be made. Descartes is correct in maintain-

[2] *Collected Papers*, 5.264–5.265.
[3] *Collected Papers*, 5.391.

ing that clear and distinct perception is an infallible guide to truth. But men are not infallible in judging whether their perceptions are clear and sufficiently distinct to provide reliable bases for belief. Most of the criticism of Descartes's rule of evidence, when it is not the result of gross misunderstanding, has been due to a failure to keep these two points distinct and to realize that the second, which Descartes understood quite well, does not undermine the first.

There are any number of passages in which Descartes acknowledges that a person may err in supposing that his perceptions are clear and distinct. "Perhaps," he tells Hobbes, "not all who suppose themselves to have [perspicuity of cognition] do have it."[4] And in replying to the Seventh Objections against his *Meditations*, he says: "Nothing can be perceived clearly and distinctly . . . that is not true. But . . . only the prudent distinguish correctly between what is perceived in that way and what merely seems or appears [to be perceived in that way]."[5] So much for Peirce's slander that this distinction never occurred to Descartes.

It was not only after his critics had suggested the need for a distinction between what is perceived clearly and distinctly and what merely seems to be so that Descartes conceded the difference between them. When he introduces his rule of evidence in Part Four of the *Discourse on Method*, which appeared several years before the *Meditations*, he says: "I came to the conclusion that I could take it as a general rule that the things we conceive very clearly and very distinctly are all true—remembering, however, that there is some difficulty in ascertaining which are those that we distinctly conceive."[6] And in the Third Meditation he confesses that he himself has at times been misled about what he perceived clearly and distinctly: "But there was something else that I affirmed, and that because of [my] habit of believing, I thought I perceived very clearly, although in fact I did not perceive it—viz., that there are things outside me. . . ."[7] Throughout his work, then, Descartes is sensitive to the risks involved in supposing that a given perception is clear and distinct.

But if Descartes merely acknowledges the distinction between seeming clear and distinct and being clear and distinct, without explaining how the distinction is to be made, then his account of

---

[4] HR II, 76; AT VII, 192, ll. 20-21.
[5] HR II, 267; AT VII, 461, l. 26—462, l. 2.
[6] HR I, 102; AT VI, 33, ll. 19-24.
[7] HR I, 158; AT VII, 35, ll. 22-26.

148

clear and distinct perception is seriously unsatisfactory. Gassendi charges it with being unsatisfactory for just this reason:

> *Nevertheless, my good Sir, notice that the difficulty seems not to be whether in order not to be deceived we ought to understand a thing clearly and distinctly, but rather by what art or method one may discern [things] in such a way that we have a clear and distinct understanding, so that it is true and it cannot be that we are deceived. For in fact we objected at the beginning that we are not infrequently deceived even though it seems to us that we cognize something so clearly and distinctly that nothing could be clearer or more distinct. Moreover, you raised this very objection against yourself, and yet we are still waiting to see this art or method to which you should be devoting your energies.*[8]

Gassendi not only accepts the rule of clarity and distinctness; he regards its acceptability as fairly obvious. "This is," he says, "not only true but true in such a way that the entire preceding Meditation, without which it could be understood, seems to have been superfluous."[9] But he objects, in effect, that the rule is unusable without a method for deciding when something really is clear and distinct.

Descartes agrees in his Reply that the method Gassendi demands is needed, but he insists that he has already provided it:

> *As regards the method by which we can distinguish the things that are really perceived clearly from those that are only thought to be perceived clearly, although I believe that this has been treated by me with sufficient care, as has already been said, still I am by no means confident that it will be easily perceived by those who work so little at stripping themselves of prejudices that they complain that I have not spoken of these matters* simply and in few words.[10]

Earlier in his Reply Descartes is somewhat more specific in indicating how he thinks he has provided the answer to Gassendi's question of method:

> *I do not dispute . . . that it is not so much a matter of having to take pains over the truth of the rule as of taking pains over a method for deciding whether or not we are deceived when we think that we perceive something clearly. But I do contend that this very thing has been carefully exhibited by me in its proper*

---

[8] HR II, 182; AT VII, 318, ll. 3-12.
[9] HR II, 182; AT VII, 318, ll. 1-3.
[10] HR II, 226; AT VII, 379, ll. 3-10.

> *place, where first I put aside all prejudices and afterwards*
> *enumerated all the principal ideas and distinguished the clear*
> *from the obscure or confused.*[11]

Just what does Descartes have in mind when he claims to have
provided the method Gassendi demands? He has in mind the illustration of his "method of rightly conducting the reason" that the
Meditations itself provides. The precepts of this method are discussed in detail in *Rules for the Direction of the Mind* (which
Descartes never published) and they are sketched in the *Discourse*.
It is possible to argue that Descartes's method is not a good one,
but it is surely not possible to pretend that he fails to take the need
for it seriously.

In offering his method, Descartes explains when it is that what
seems clear and distinct may properly be taken to be so: when the
rules of his method have been conscientiously and correctly followed. His method is, in fact, a method for getting into a position
in which what seems clear and distinct is actually so. Only after a
person has performed the analyses, made the distinctions, and conducted the careful reviews that the Cartesian method prescribes, is
it reasonable for him to decide that his apparently clear and distinct
perception really is clear and distinct. The rules of Descartes's
method are precisely the rules Gassendi demands. They constitute
an account of the ideal conditions for clear and distinct perception.
When these conditions are satisfied, what seems clear and distinct
and what is clear and distinct coincide.

The method may, of course, be misused; perceptions may be
supposed to occur under ideal conditions when in fact they do not.
The statement that a certain perception is clear and distinct must
always be regarded, therefore, as a hypothesis that is subject to
correction. It may be entertained more or less diffidently as there
is a greater or lesser chance that the conditions for clear and distinct
perception have been fulfilled. There is no absurdity in the consequence that evidence may be demanded for the statement that
something is clearly and distinctly perceived. The evidence will
concern the conditions under which the perception occurs. To give
such evidence, however, is not the same as to give evidence for the
proposition perceived. There is, accordingly, no conflict with Descartes's claim that clear and distinct perception is itself a conclusive
basis for belief.

There is a story that the mathematician G. H. Hardy, in going

[11] HR II, 214; AT VII, 361, l. 23—362, l. 4.

through a proof one day with some students, referred to a certain step in his argument as self-evident and passed over it without any further comment. A student complained that he could not "see" the step in question. Hardy then took another look at it and found that he could not "see" it either; whereupon he retreated into his study and worked furiously for some time, covering sheet after sheet of paper with calculations and analyses. Finally he emerged and announced: "I was right. It *is* self-evident!" Descartes's theory of clear and distinct perception is not strictly a theory of self-evidence, but the story is nonetheless apposite. There is no paradox in Hardy's claim to have discovered, after a great deal of work, that something is self-evident. And there is no paradox in Descartes's notion that it may require a considerable investigation to determine whether or not a certain perception is really clear and distinct.

Descartes is no more impressed than anyone else would be by the fact that something seems clear and distinct to a fool or to a person who is in no position to know what he is talking about. But he recognizes that there is no alternative to accepting the report of a rational perceiver whose perception occurs under the best conditions possible. While it is not reasonable to decide that a perception is clear and distinct simply because it seems so, it is unreasonable *not* to make this decision if the perception seems clear and distinct in circumstances that are ideal for clear and distinct perception. The situation is analogous to one that is familiar in the realm of sense perception. The fact that an object looks red to someone at some time, or that a pointer seems to be in a certain position on a dial, is not conclusive evidence that the object is red or that the pointer is in that position. But suppose that the light is good, the observer has normal vision, and he examines the object in question attentively from close by. In that case it is only reasonable to reject the observer's testimony if all testimony concerning what is visually observable is to be dismissed. For no observations can reasonably be regarded as more reliable than those made by an ideal observer under ideal conditions.

The criteria of clarity and distinctness themselves have nothing essentially to do with any state of consciousness. The application of these criteria, however, does of course involve recognizing whether or not they are satisfied in a particular case. In the end the inquirer must say to himself whether he believes that they are. Exactly the same thing is true of *any* rule of evidence. Peirce and other critics of Descartes tend to ignore the difference between relying irresponsibly upon casual impressions and relying ultimately upon what appears to be the case after a disciplined and rigorous attempt to get into a position in which appearances can be trusted.

It is no part of Descartes's doctrine that errors concerning what is clear and distinct may not be made even when all reasonable precautions have apparently been taken. What is clearly and distinctly perceived is certainly true, Descartes maintains, but he does not claim it is ever certain that a given perception is actually clear and distinct. The statement that a given perception is so is to be regarded as a hypothesis—a hypothesis as corrigible as any pragmaticist could desire. It may well be that the proposition that *p* is clearly and distinctly perceived is not itself clearly and distinctly perceived. Descartes is fully aware of this. It creates a problem for the theory of knowledge and of inquiry, but the problem it creates besets any theory, not just Descartes's.

My discussion of clarity and distinctness has focused almost exclusively on the logical aspects of Descartes's rule of evidence. It may have given the impression that clear and distinct perception is primarily a discursive or analytical affair; it may have suggested that clarity is achieved only by analyzing the relation between a proposition and its evidential basis in order to determine whether or not any grounds for doubting the proposition are still conceivable, and that distinctness requires a process of distinguishing the proposition in question from others with which it might be confused. These logical aspects need to be emphasized because the rule is so often misunderstood as giving a merely psychological or "subjective" account of evidence. There is a psychological element in Descartes's doctrine, however, which must now be considered.

There is a difference between having a clear and distinct perception and being able to show that a perception is clear and distinct. The latter necessarily requires analysis and argument but the former does not. A proposition cannot be clearly and distinctly perceived unless certain logical relationships obtain, and to establish that a perception is clear and distinct requires, therefore, an examination of these relationships. But a person may "see" that "Socrates is mortal" follows from "If Socrates is a man then Socrates is mortal; and Socrates is a man" without either spelling out the form of the argument or demonstrating the validity of *modus ponens.*

Consider a case in which a person with a toothache perceives clearly and distinctly that he is in pain. The evidential basis constituted by his feeling enables him to perceive clearly and distinctly, but he does not need to demonstrate to himself by any process of argument that what he feels makes it inconceivable that the proposition is false. His perception that he is in pain is quite immediate; only if he wishes to explain or to test its clarity and distinctness must he resort to explicit logical procedures.

When a proposition is not so directly and transparently tied to its evidential basis, clear and distinct perception may be impossible without some considerable preliminary application of the rules of Descartes's method. The strength of logical intuition and acumen varies from one person to another. There can be no definitive classification, accordingly, of propositions that can and cannot be clearly and distinctly perceived without making a systematic effort to connect them with their evidential bases. The axioms of a formal calculus provide an evidential basis for the clear and distinct perception of its theorems, but the fact that some complicated theorem is conclusively established by the axioms is not something that most people can "see" as readily as they can "see" that they are in pain. Most people must do some work to make the relation between the theorem and the axioms apparent to them.

Since it is not by using the familiar organs of sense perception that clear and distinct perception is accomplished, Descartes's theory has struck some critics as rather mysterious or even a bit occult: the faculty of vision operates through the eyes, but what is the organ through which the natural light of reason functions? But this question raises no philosophical difficulty. The mechanics of Descartes's "perception" is a subject for psychologists to study. For his purposes, it is sufficient to identify the phenomenon that he has in mind and to assure himself that it does occur.

At least two relatively recent developments have encouraged a tendency among many philosophers to overlook the role of intuition in reasoning: the extensive formalization of logic, together with the creation of more or less mechanical techniques of logical calculation; and the evidence that counter-intuitive logical principles are viable. But however it is that logical principles may be established, and whatever their ultimate justification, the use of any such principles (either within a calculus or in the application of a calculus to a subject matter) is impossible without what it is quite natural and convenient to refer to as a kind of "seeing." Even if it can be established in an entirely mechanical way that arguments of a certain form are acceptable, it is still necessary to determine that a given argument is of this form before the principle in question can be used in reasoning.

Suppose that someone considers the familiar argument concerning the mortality of Socrates. He may know that the following is a valid argument form: If p then q; p; therefore, q. Perhaps he can attain this knowledge without relying at all upon intuition. But how is he to determine that the argument about Socrates is of this form, if not simply by seeing that it is? Formal logic may define the conditions in which conclusions may reasonably be drawn, but it cannot decide when these conditions have been satisfied. It is difficult to understand how this kind of decision can be made without relying on something nonformal—without a perception that the conditions defined by the rules in question prevail. My point is not to suggest that clear and distinct perception is uniquely a matter of discerning logical forms, but rather to locate or identify the familiar experience that is involved in every clear and distinct perception: the grasping of a logical relationship.

When Descartes talks about the occurrence of clear and distinct perceptions he has in mind situations in which a person finds something so evident that he cannot help believing it. There are, to be sure, many such situations in which there is no clear and distinct perception at all; but an irresistible inclination to believe is an invariable result of clear and distinct perception. "Our mind is of such a nature," Descartes affirms, "that it cannot fail to assent to things that are clearly understood."[12] "We are by nature so disposed to give our assent to things that we clearly perceive," he insists, "that we cannot possibly doubt their truth."[13] The fact that a person finds himself unable to doubt something does not show that his perception is actually a clear and distinct one; but if it is clear and distinct, he will be unable to doubt what he perceives.

Seeing is believing, and if it were not, then the enterprise of inquiry would be altogether impossible except as an exercise in free choice. For the irresistibility of the clear and distinct is what breaks into the potentially disastrous regress implicit in the use of any criterion of evidence. Descartes's rule is to accept as true only what he perceives clearly and distinctly. His problem is to know what he in fact so perceives. Must he clearly and distinctly perceive, then, that a given perception is clear and distinct? Then what about this

[12] Letter to Regius, 24 May 1640, AT III, 64, ll. 24-25.
[13] *Principles of Philosophy*, I, xliii; AT VIII, 21, ll. 17-19.

second perception, or the third perception that might be invoked to validate the second?

The regress does not subvert the claim that what is clear and distinct is true. Left unchecked, however, it does subvert all confidence in distinguishing clear and distinct perceptions from their deceptive counterfeits. What is not clearly and distinctly perceived can be doubted. If what is clearly and distinctly perceived can *also* be doubted, how could there be an end to doubt that would not be entirely arbitrary and capricious? If nothing satisfies us, we can at best pretend to be satisfied and agree to suffer the lingering disgust with ourselves that self-deception inevitably evokes.

Theories of self-evidence generally hold that there are certain propositions whose truth is infallibly recognized whenever they are considered. Descartes does maintain that various elementary necessary propositions have this characteristic, but his theory of clear and distinct perception is not equivalent to this claim. It is not a theory that there is a specifiable set of irreducibly trustworthy propositions, but a theory that there are irreducibly trustworthy circumstances. These circumstances are defined by the rules of his method. The idea of a proper subset of true propositions that can be perceived clearly and distinctly is altogether absurd from his point of view, since any true proposition (excluding certain mysteries of religious dogma) may be the object of a clear and distinct perception.

What Descartes says about clear and distinct perception is, as I have already suggested, analogous to what almost anyone would say about vision or about other forms of sensory experience. The claim that the senses can contribute to knowledge does not mean that there is a specific set of propositions concerning sensory objects that must be acknowledged as true by anyone who considers them. No one supposes that there are. But it is generally accepted that there are certain circumstances, involving the use of the senses, in which what seems irresistibly to be the case actually is the case. If this were not so, the use of the senses in inquiry would not be possible. Descartes makes a similar point concerning the non-sensory logical relationships upon which any rational conception of evidence must depend.

MEMORY
AND DOUBT

Once Descartes has formulated the principle of clarity and distinctness, his task is to determine whether or not it is an acceptable rule of evidence. Now perceiving clearly and distinctly is an activity of the reason. It is what the faculty of reason does when it is at its best. The problem of deciding whether clear and distinct perceptions can be trusted, therefore, is the problem of validating reason. Descartes's way of dealing with this problem is well known. He demonstrates that there is a being—God—who is both omnipotent and benign. And then from the fact that God is benevolent and hence not a deceiver, he infers that the truth of what is clearly and distinctly perceived has a divine guarantee.

Descartes's procedure in this matter has struck many critics as outrageously defective, and one can easily see why. His arguments for God's existence and veracity proceed from premises that are guaranteed by nothing but the clarity and distinctness with which he perceives them. Thus it seems that he cannot demonstrate that there is a divine guarantee of reason unless he first assumes that the reason can be trusted. His arguments apparently rely upon the very faculty of reason whose reliability is presumably at stake, and his attempt to validate clear and distinct perception therefore seems to be vitiated by circularity. It is tempting to suppose, indeed, that *any* such attempt *must* be circular. To give reasons in behalf of reason seems a transparently fallacious procedure, which inevitably begs the question of whether reason is reliable.

Some of Descartes's critics have insisted, accordingly, that the only way to absolve him of committing an elementary logical blunder is to find that he was not trying to provide a justification of reason at all. In an effort to find a way out of the "Cartesian circle," they have suggested that the object of the metaphysical doubt to which Descartes's demon hypothesis gives rise is not the reliability of reason but of memory. Their motivation is the belief that validating reason is so palpably an impossible task that it ought not to be ascribed to Descartes if a less damaging way of understanding him can be found. But the memory thesis is in fact contradicted by what Descartes himself says, and does not even succeed in enabling him to escape from the charge of circularity. In any event, that his attempt to validate reason suffers from the ascribed logical defect is not so evident as it may seem.

Those who endorse the memory thesis claim that Descartes makes no attempt to determine whether what is clearly and distinctly perceived is true. He is only interested, according to them, in providing grounds for trusting recollections of what has been clearly and distinctly perceived. In a long process of reasoning it becomes necessary to recall what was clearly and distinctly perceived at earlier stages. A difficulty arises here because memory is fallible, and the memory thesis maintains that it is this difficulty Descartes seeks to remove by proving the existence of a veracious God. If the memory thesis is correct, Descartes never doubts that what is clearly and distinctly perceived is true. His metaphysical doubt concerns simply the possibility that the demon victimizes us by making us think we remember clearly and distinctly perceiving what we in fact never clearly and distinctly perceived at all.

This thesis appears to commit Descartes to the absurd doctrine that memory is infallible, at least in cases where memory reports that something was clearly and distinctly perceived. The accuracy of a recollection that something has been established by clear and distinct perception is guaranteed, according to the memory thesis, by the veracity of God. The thesis seems to mean, then, that Descartes believes all doubts about the reliability of such memories are legitimately dispelled by the awareness that a veracious God exists. But Descartes certainly cannot have accepted so incredible a doctrine. He cannot have believed that all memories of clear and distinct perceptions—no matter in what circumstances and no matter how long after the events they recall—can be accepted with absolute confidence. He surely knew as well as everyone else does that memory sometimes misleads or deceives us.

In fact it is easy to show that even after he has proved God's existence and veracity, Descartes still does not regard the reports of memory as having any special guarantee. In *Principles of Philosophy*, for instance, he demonstrates God's existence and veracity in Principles 14, 18, and 21 of Part One. Yet in Principle 44 of Part

One, he says that "we very often err, however, in that we suppose that many things have once been perceived by us and, trusting to memory, we assent to those things as if they had indeed been perceived, although in fact we never did perceive them."[1] Thus he reaffirms the very doubt that, according to the memory thesis, he has removed by proving God's existence. Neither in this nor in subsequent passages, moreover, does he retract or qualify his warning about memory.

It is rather difficult to know how to formulate the memory thesis in a plausible way. One of its advocates says: "memory being fallible, God must vindicate its use."[2] But if memory is actually fallible, how can it be vindicated, by God or in any other way? If it is really vindicated by God, on the other hand, how can it be fallible? Perhaps the memory thesis is to be understood differently, so that God's guarantee of memory is not supposed to entail that all memories of clear and distinct perceptions are accurate. Perhaps it is to be understood as entailing only the weaker proposition that memory is not an insurmountably treacherous faculty, i.e., that some memories are trustworthy and that we are capable of distinguishing these from those that are not. On this weaker construction the memory thesis is by no means outlandish, and Descartes's warnings about memory are not inconsistent with it. They can be understood as warning only against the indiscriminate acceptance of memory reports and as recommending that care be exercised in distinguishing reliable memories from unreliable ones.

But does the memory thesis, either in its stronger or weaker version, actually extricate Descartes's reasoning from its apparent circularity? Given that he relies on God's existence just to guarantee the reliability of memory, Descartes's reasoning will be free of circularity only if his proof of God's existence does not itself require the use of memory. Now Descartes does think it possible for certain demonstrations to be carried out without any dependence on memory. He claims that when a demonstration is fairly short and simple it is possible that, perhaps after a little practice, the entire proof can be brought to mind in one encompassing perception. In such a case, all the steps can be present to the mind at once and there need be no reliance on memory.

Descartes evidently thinks that the reasoning by which he dem-

---

[1] HR I, 236; AT VIII, 21.
[2] Willis Doney, "The Cartesian Circle," *Journal of the History of Ideas*, XVI (1955), 326.

onstrates God's existence is short enough and simple enough to be accomplished without memory.[3] But it would not be sufficient for him, whenever he requires God's guarantee, merely to recall that he has worked out this demonstration. It is precisely this sort of recollection, after all, whose dependability is in doubt when the guarantee is invoked. To assume the accuracy of such a recollection would therefore be to generate a new circle. When he doubts the reliability of memory Descartes must necessarily doubt the reliability of his recollection that he has shown memory to be guaranteed by God. It would clearly be circular for him to offer as a validation of memory the fact that he remembers having proved that God guarantees memory.

Can this new circle be avoided? It would be avoided if, whenever Descartes needs to invoke the divine guarantee of memory, he brings to mind the entire demonstration of the guarantee. Simply recalling the steps in this demonstration will not suffice; he must attend to each of them, and to their relations to one another, with all the concentration needed for clear and distinct perception. When he is conducting the sort of demonstration in which he needs the divine guarantee, therefore, he must simultaneously not only attend to the current step in his proof and keep in mind what steps he is recalling; he must also perceive clearly and distinctly all the steps in the demonstration that God exists and all in the demonstration that God validates the use of memory. Descartes does think it possible to attend to more than one thing at a time, but it is not so clear that he accepts the possibility of performing this kind of intellectual juggling act. Yet the memory thesis requires him either to believe that it is performed whenever a long and complex demonstration is properly conducted, or else to fall into a new fallacy of circularity.

Descartes would in any case be guilty of this new circularity if the memory thesis were actually correct. For he explains in the *Meditations* that he does *not* think it necessary to attend to the demonstration of God's existence and veracity whenever he invokes the divine guarantee. Near the end of the Fifth Meditation, he says:

> *But after I have perceived that there is a God ... and from that have concluded that all those things that I perceive clearly and distinctly are necessarily true then, even if I attend no further to*

[3] AT V, 148-149; Charles Adam, ed., *Entretien avec Burman* (Paris: Boivin, 1937), pp. 9-13.

> *the reasons for which I judged that this was true, just as long as*
> *I recall that I did perceive clearly and distinctly, no contrary*
> *reason can be brought forward that could drive me to doubt;*
> *rather, I have true and certain knowledge of it.*[4]

Descartes insists, then, that it is sufficient simply to recollect that God's existence and veracity have been demonstrated. Accordingly, if the memory thesis is accepted, he is easily convicted of the blunder of relying upon recollection to provide evidence for the reliability of recollection. Thus the memory thesis generates the very defect it is designed to remove.

If there were unmistakable textual support for the memory thesis, it would be necessary to acknowledge that Descartes falls into the difficulties with which the thesis burdens him. In fact, however, there is no clear and direct evidence for it. The passages in which Descartes attempts to answer the charge of circularity do indicate that memory has *something* to do with the problem he tries to solve by proving God's existence, but nothing in them requires the memory thesis concerning the exact relevance of memory to his argument.

There is very strong textual evidence, on the other hand, that his metaphysical doubt is not one about memory. A careful examination of certain important passages indicates that, far from being the object of the metaphysical doubt, the reliability of memory must be assumed in order for the doubt to arise. Here, for instance, is a passage from Descartes's Reply to the Second Objections:

> *There are other things that are indeed also perceived very*
> *clearly by our intellect, when we attend sufficiently to the reasons*
> *on which the cognition of them depends, and as a consequence*
> *we cannot be in doubt about them at this time. But since we can*
> *forget those reasons and meanwhile remember the conclusions*
> *deduced from them, the question arises whether there is a firm*
> *and immutable persuasion regarding those conclusions as long*
> *as we remember that they have been deduced from evident princi-*
> *ples (for this recollection must be supposed in order for them to*
> *be called conclusions). And I answer that [such a firm and immu-*
> *table persuasion] is indeed the possession of those who know God*
> *in such a way that they understand that the faculty of under-*
> *standing given them by him must tend toward truth.*[5]

The accuracy of the recollection is taken for granted, as Descartes

[4] HR I, 184; AT VII, 70.
[5] HR II, 42-43; AT VII, 146, ll. 14–26.

himself points out. If it were not taken for granted, there would be no occasion to doubt at all.

Descartes's problem is not whether memory is reliable, but whether *what* is recollected—that something was deduced from principles that were evident—is sufficient to establish the truth of the conclusion in question. What he doubts is whether the remembered fact that *p* was proved at a certain time entitles him to be certain at a later time of *p*'s truth. God is not invoked to guarantee the reliability of memory. In fact, the reliability of memory must be accepted in order to generate the doubt that God is called upon to dispel.

There is further confirmation, in the *Conversation with Burman*, of the view that Descartes assumes the reliability of memory in his attempt to remove the metaphysical doubt. After reviewing Descartes's discussion of God's veracity, Burman says:

> *But, someone may say, after I have demonstrated that there is a God and that he is not a deceiver I can say not, indeed, that intelligence deceives me (since I have received that direct from God), but that memory deceives me. For I seem to recall something that in actual fact I do not recall, since [memory] itself is feeble.*[6]

Descartes makes the following reply to Burman's remarks:

> *I can say nothing about memory, for each person must test himself to see whether he has a good memory. And if he has any doubt about it, he has at his disposal writing and such devices, which will help him.*

If Descartes had intended his proof of the existence of a veracious God to establish the reliability of memory, he would surely not have responded in this way to Burman. He would have pointed out that the doubts Burman expresses about memory have already been dealt with by his proof. Burman clearly brings up doubt about memory as something that has not yet been considered, even though the proof that a veracious God exists has already been accomplished. He is calling attention to what he regards as a new difficulty. Descartes's agreement that the difficulty remains is clear from the fact that he does not deny it, and from the fact that he offers instead a rather commonsensical bit of advice, recommending routine caution and the use of mnemonic devices. These are hardly the responses of a man who regards the reliability of memory as a basic metaphysical problem, much less as one he has recently

[6] AT V, 148; *Entretien avec Burman*, p. 9.

solved. They suggest vividly that Descartes's attention is focused on quite different matters, in which the problem of the reliability of memory is of only incidental concern.

The memory thesis, then, is both false and unhelpful. It is inconsistent with Descartes's account of his views and does not satisfactorily allow him to escape the charge of circularity. Descartes does sometimes describe the problem with which he is concerned as one that may be encountered in contexts in which something is remembered, but even in such contexts his problem is not to establish the reliability of memory. It is to validate propositions that are correctly remembered to have been clearly and distinctly perceived.

Suppose that two weeks ago, in the course of studying a geometry text, a person clearly and distinctly perceived that p; and suppose this person now correctly recalls having had that perception. Descartes wants to know whether the person is justified in accepting p as certainly true—whether, that is, he should accept as conclusive evidence of p's truth the fact that he once perceived clearly and distinctly that p. His answer is that the person is justified if he knows that God exists, but not otherwise: "In order for us to be certain that something is true it suffices that we remember that we have perceived it clearly; this would not suffice if we did not know that there is a God and that he does not deceive us."[7]

Often hindering a correct understanding of Descartes's problem is the erroneous notion that when he says something is indubitable, this is tantamount to his saying it is true. Despite the fact that his metaphysical labors are largely devoted to exploring the relations between what is indubitable and what is true, it is not at all uncommon to find able writers on his work apparently overlooking the distinction between them. For example, in the course of discussing the account of mathematical propositions in the First Meditation, Leonard Miller remarks: "Descartes is puzzled by the nature of these propositions whose truth appears to be self-evident, for he is inclined to say both that we cannot possibly be mistaken about them provided that we apprehend them clearly and distinctly and that we can be deceived by the demon no matter how clearly and distinctly we perceive them."[8]

But on what evidence does Miller ascribe to Descartes the view that even if there is a demon we cannot be mistaken about what we

[7] HR II, 45; AT VII, 246, ll. 7-9.
[8] Leonard Miller, "Descartes, Mathematics, and God," *Philosophical Review*, LXVI (1957), 452.

perceive clearly and distinctly? The only evidence he cites is to the effect that what is clearly and distinctly perceived is not dubitable[9] —as if in saying (as he wishes to do) that we cannot doubt what we are clearly and distinctly perceiving, Descartes is also saying (as he does not wish to do) that we cannot be in error about what we are clearly and distinctly perceiving but know it to be true whether or not we know that God exists. There may be more adequate evidence for Miller's statement, but that is not to the point. To show that Descartes believes it impossible (demon or no demon) to *err* about what is clearly and distinctly perceived, it is not appropriate merely to show that he thinks it impossible (demon or no demon) to *doubt* what is being clearly and distinctly perceived.

According to Willis Doney, similarly, Descartes claims that even without knowing God's existence a person can know that what he at present clearly and distinctly perceives is true: "Present clear and distinct perceptions were never subject to doubt. Anything so perceived did not depend on God as guarantor of its truth."[10] Notice how readily Doney moves from speaking of something clearly and distinctly perceived as not subject to doubt, to speaking of it as known to be true. He too evidently assumes that if something clearly and distinctly perceived is not subject to doubt, that is the same as its being known to be true. This explains why he regards the second of the two statements I have quoted from his essay as established by the truth of the first. Here again, the point is not that what he says is false, but that the relation between his statements is not what he supposes it to be.

Descartes's metaphysical doubt is precisely a doubt about whether being false is compatible with being indubitable. His position is that as long as he regards the existence of a demon as possible, he must acknowledge that what he perceives clearly and distinctly may be false. But he also holds that he cannot doubt the truth of what he perceives while he is perceiving it clearly and distinctly. "Our mind is of such a nature," he says, "that it cannot refuse to assent to what it apprehends clearly."[11] Descartes enunciates this doctrine on a number of occasions,[12] but never explains his grounds for it. He sometimes gives the impression that it is simply

---

[9] See *ibid.*, pp. 451-452.
[10] Willis Doney, "The Cartesian Circle," *Journal of the History of Ideas*, XVI (1955), 325-326.
[11] Letter to Regius, 24 May 1640, AT III, 64.
[12] See HR I, 160; AT VII, 38; and *Principles of Philosophy*, Part I, Principle 43.

a fact that the clear and distinct is irresistible. We are, he observes, disposed to find it so "by nature." This may suggest that our inability to withhold belief is like a moth's inability to keep away from a flame or like our overwhelming inclination to laugh when we are tickled. If it is in this sense that nature impels us to assent, then the fact that we do so is just an accident of our psychology.[13]

Descartes maintains that we are led by nature to believe not only what we perceive clearly and distinctly but also some other things as well. The belief that our ideas resemble objects external to our minds, for instance, is one to which he says we are impelled by "a certain spontaneous inclination."[14] But *this* inclination is *not* confirmed by the natural light of reason and, unlike those that accompany clear and distinct perceptions, it *is* resistible. It can be withstood, in fact, by anyone who recognizes it to be a matter of blind impulse rather than a response to conclusive evidence. Such a person can find a reasonable ground for doubt and can thereby successfully resist the inclination to believe.

To perceive something clearly and distinctly, however, is to be aware of grounds for believing it so complete that no basis for doubt remains. In the case of a clear and distinct perception, all possible doubts are already resolved by what is being perceived. It is therefore no mere accident or brute contingency that a person cannot help believing what he perceives clearly and distinctly. It is only reasonable that he should be unable to withhold his belief, because he has the best possible basis for assenting. If he is unwilling to be satisfied by this, then reason clearly cannot satisfy him at all. Hence it is not only reasonable to assent to what is being clearly and distinctly perceived; it is, as Descartes suggests, also in a sense natural. A human life in which reason played no practical role whatever—in which a person's intellectual inclinations were unaffected by his evaluations of evidence—may be a formal possibility. But it would not be implausible to regard such a life as unnatural. Whether or not this is the appropriate direction in which to go for an explanation of Descartes's doctrine concerning the relation between clear and distinct perception and assent, the doctrine itself is clear. (There is a rather obvious analogy between Descartes's notion that the will is constrained by clear and distinct perception

[13] See Jean Laporte, *Le rationalisme de Descartes* (Paris: Presses Universitaires de France, 1950), p. 172.
[14] HR I, 160; AT VII, 38.

and the doctrine of some classical philosophers that desire is constrained by perception of the good.)

While the perception lasts, the inclination to believe what is being perceived clearly and distinctly is irresistible; no doubt is then possible. But doubt may well arise at other times, if God's existence is unknown. "Before someone knows that God exists," Descartes declares, "he has an occasion for being in doubt about everything (viz., about everything of which he does not have a clear perception present in his mind, as I have explained a number of times)."[15]

Now at a time when we are having no clear and distinct perceptions, we may recall having once perceived something clearly and distinctly. Descartes maintains that if we know that God exists we are entitled to accept the fact that something was once clearly and distinctly perceived as conclusively establishing its truth. The recollection then suffices to establish the truth of what we remember perceiving. But if God's existence is not known, he claims, we must suspect that what we remember perceiving clearly and distinctly may be false even though we once clearly and distinctly perceived it and were at that time incapable of doubting it. For without the knowledge of God, "I can persuade myself that nature has made me in such a way that I am from time to time deceived in things that I suppose I perceive in the most evident way possible."[16] Thus the fact that we find something to be indubitable—our apprehending it "in the most evident way possible"—cannot be regarded as itself a sufficient sign of truth. On the contrary, as long as we are ignorant of God's existence we must fear that it may be due to the malice of a demon who delights in making us find error irresistible.

In the passage just quoted, Descartes speaks of matters that he *supposes* himself to apprehend with great evidence and certainty, and not simply of matters that he does thus apprehend; and in other passages, which will be quoted below, he speaks of things that *seem* to him most manifest, matters that he *regards* himself as perceiving clearly and distinctly, or things that he *believes* himself to be apprehending clearly. But this hardly jeopardizes the point that Descartes does not assume that whatever is indubitable is true. For if he did assume it, then whenever he believed himself to have perceived something clearly and distinctly, it would be reasonable for

---

[15] HR II, 333; AT VII, 546, ll. 22-26.
[16] HR I, 184; AT VII, 70.

him to think that what he believed himself to have perceived is true. He says repeatedly, however, that even when he does think that something has been perceived clearly and distinctly, he must nonetheless acknowledge that it may be false (assuming he does not know of God's existence).

Although it may appear to do so, Descartes's doctrine does not commit him to the view that before God's existence is known any proposition can be doubted. For he carefully leaves open the possibility that there are propositions so simple that they cannot be thought of at all without being clearly and distinctly perceived. Such propositions could never be doubted by anyone, with or without a knowledge of God's existence. For no one could doubt them without thinking of them, and anyone who thought of them would perceive them clearly and distinctly and would hence be unable to doubt them. Descartes maintains explicitly that there are such propositions, and he regards an analogue of the *cogito* as one of them.

> *Of those [things] that are perceived clearly by the [intellect] some are so evident and at the same time so simple that we can never think about them without believing that they are true—e.g., that I, while I am thinking, exist; that things that are once done cannot be undone, and the like. . . . For we cannot be in doubt about them unless we think about them, but we cannot think about them without at the same time believing that they are true. . . . Therefore we cannot be in doubt about them without at the same time believing that they are true—i.e., we cannot ever be in doubt [about them].*[17]

Now Descartes repeatedly asserts, without any qualification or limitation whatever, that as long as he is ignorant of God's existence he must fear that a proposition may be false even though he perceives it quite clearly and distinctly.[18] He does not exempt the *cogito* (or its analogues) from his general concern that unless God exists, even what is perceived clearly and distinctly may be false. Until the rule of clarity and distinctness is validated, the relation between the indubitability of the *cogito* and its truth is problematic. The *cogito* is so simple that it cannot be thought of without being clearly and distinctly perceived and hence found irresistible. But the fact that it can never be doubted is not identical with its being true or with its being known to be true. Descartes can still wonder

[17] HR II, 42; AT VII, 145, l. 22—146, l. 4.
[18] See HR I, 184; also HR I, 158-159; AT VII, 70; AT VII, 36.

166

whether its indubitability, however inescapable, is sufficient to establish its truth.

Near the beginning of the Third Meditation, in the course of discussing why it is essential for him to inquire into the existence and nature of God, Descartes explains the metaphysical doubt to which he is still subject. This doubt is aroused, he says, by considering the possibility that

> *perhaps some God could have endowed me with such a nature that I would be deceived even about those things that seemed most manifest. . . . It is easy for him, if he wishes, to cause me to err even in those things that I suppose myself to behold with the eyes of the mind in the most evident way possible.*[19]

This statement is clear evidence that Descartes is concerned with the possibility that even what is perceived clearly and distinctly may be false.

What he says immediately afterwards, however, may appear to conflict with my interpretation:

> *Whenever I turn my attention to those things that I think I perceive very clearly, I am so entirely persuaded by them that I find myself saying: Let anyone who can do so deceive me, but he will never bring it about . . . that 2 and 3 added together are more or less than 5; or bring about anything of the sort in which I recognize a manifest inconsistency.*[20]

It is in fact quite easy to reconcile this statement with my claim that Descartes wonders whether even what is being clearly and distinctly perceived may not be false. He does not say that no one could bring it about that he is deceived about the sum of 2 and 3 or about other things that he apprehends clearly. He only says that while apprehending them clearly, he is "so entirely persuaded" of their truth that he cannot help saying that he cannot be deceived about them. The fact that he is so strongly persuaded of their truth is not the same as their being true; nor is his inability at the time to conceive that he is mistaken the same as his being in fact free of error. In this passage Descartes describes the convictions that he is irresistibly inclined to hold under certain circumstances, and he reports the assertions that he feels confidently disposed under these circumstances to make. But he does not say either that the convictions are reasonable or that the assertions are true.

The relevance of memory in Descartes's metaphysical doubt, and

[19] HR I, 158-159; AT VII, 36.
[20] *Ibid.*

the general nature of the doubt, are made clear in this passage from his Reply to the Second Objections:

> *There are other things that are indeed also perceived very clearly by our intellect when we attend sufficiently to the reasons on which the cognition of them depends, and as a consequence we cannot be in doubt about them at that time. But since we can forget those reasons and meanwhile remember the conclusions deduced from them, the question arises whether there is a firm and immutable persuasion regarding those conclusions as long as we remember that they have been deduced from evident principles (for this recollection must be supposed in order for them to be called conclusions). And I answer that [such a firm and immutable persuasion] is indeed the possession of those who know God in such a way that they understand that the faculty of understanding given them by Him must tend toward truth.*[21]

Descartes is supposing that someone once deduced a conclusion from premises that he perceived clearly and distinctly at the time, but that the person no longer remembers the premises. Thus the person does not now clearly and distinctly perceive that his conclusion follows from premises that he is presently perceiving clearly and distinctly. He only remembers that the premises were evident to him at one time (i.e., that he once perceived them clearly and distinctly) and that he deduced the conclusion from them (i.e., once perceived clearly and distinctly that the conclusion follows from them).

While he was clearly and distinctly perceiving the premises, Descartes maintains, he was not able to doubt them; nor was he able to doubt that the conclusion follows from the premises while he was perceiving its relation to them clearly and distinctly. But now he is free to doubt these things. His problem is to decide whether doubt is justified or whether what he remembers suffices to establish the soundness of the argument he is considering. The question is this: Given that a proposition has been clearly and distinctly perceived to follow from premises that were themselves perceived clearly and distinctly, is it possible that the proposition should be false? Is it possible, in other words, that a proposition should be perceived clearly and distinctly to follow from a set of premises— i.e., be deduced from the set—without actually following from it? And is it possible that premises should be evident—i.e., be perceived so clearly and distinctly as to be subject at the time to no

[21] HR II, 42-43; AT VII, 146, ll. 14-26.

doubt at all—without being true?

The metaphysical doubt arises for Descartes when he remembers some clear and distinct perception, but it is not a doubt about the reliability of memory. Indeed there is no reason why metaphysical doubt may not arise even in situations in which there is no recollection of anything being perceived. A suitable context for the doubt is provided by any set of circumstances in which a person can consider the validity of clear and distinct perception, and these circumstances need not involve any recollections of clear and distinct perceptions. Thus suppose that at a certain time one man *A* perceives something clearly and distinctly, and that another man *B* knows right then and there that *A* is doing so. Suppose further that *B* is uncertain whether the occurrence of *A*'s clear and distinct perception is sufficient to establish the truth of what *A* is perceiving. Then *B* is engaging in metaphysical doubt about what *A* is perceiving, and it is evident that *B* need not be remembering anything at all while doing so.

Descartes's failure to make this altogether clear is not difficult to explain. When he discusses these matters in the *Meditations*, his metaphysics is still so undeveloped that he does not know that anyone exists but himself. He does not, accordingly, consider any perceptions but his own. Since he cannot doubt the validity of his own clear and distinct perceptions while they are occurring, he can engage in metaphysical doubt about them only after they have occurred and while he recollects their occurrence. Metaphysical doubt arises in the *Meditations*, therefore, only when Descartes recollects having perceived something clearly and distinctly. But this is due to the order in which he takes up matters in the *Meditations*, and not to the nature of his doubt itself.

Given that Descartes is indeed trying to validate reason by showing that what is perceived clearly and distinctly is true, it is still necessary to consider more closely just what is at stake in his metaphysical doubt. Following the realistic bias of common sense, it is rather natural to assume that when he asks whether what is clear and distinct is true, Descartes is asking whether it corresponds with reality. This assumption is not correct. In fact, as I will show, Descartes says explicitly that he is not interested in this correspondence.

In seeking to understand what Descartes is after in his validation of reason, and to evaluate the cogency of his argument, it is useful to recall his procedure in determining the reliability of the senses in the First Meditation. The trouble he found there with sensory evidence was that the senses might, for all he knew, provide conflicting testimony: his basis for rejecting the rules of sensory evidence was essentially that someone following these rules might conceivably be led to accept inconsistent evidence. Now it is reasonable to suppose that when he considers reason, Descartes wishes to discover whether the rule of reason—the principle of clear and distinct perception—passes the test that the rules of sensory evidence have already failed.

This illuminates what question about reason Descartes finds it necessary to ask and how he thinks it possible to give a reasonable answer. The presumption that his attempt to validate reason parallels his attempt to validate the senses suggests that what he wants to know about clear and distinct perceptions is whether they are consistent with one another. The conception of truth involved in his question about the truth of what is clearly and distinctly perceived is, in other words, a conception of *coherence* rather than of *correspondence.* When it is understood that his problem is to remove any basis for doubting the consistency of the set of clear and distinct perceptions, it is not so difficult to understand how his argument avoids the elementary logical blunder of circularity with which it has so often been charged.

One of the first to be struck by the apparent circularity of Descartes's reasoning was Arnauld, who made the point as follows:

> It is manifest to us that the things perceived clearly and distinctly by us are true only because there is a God. But it can be manifest to us that there is a God only because that is perceived clearly and distinctly by us. Therefore, before it is manifest to us that there is a God it must be manifest to us that whatever is perceived clearly and distinctly by us is true.[1]

If the fact that something is manifest to us means that we are unable to doubt it, then God's existence can be manifest to us even if we do not yet know that whatever is perceived clearly and distinctly is true. For if we perceive that God's existence follows from premisses that are at the same time also clearly and distinctly perceived, then while these perceptions occur we will be unable to doubt that God exists even if we do not know that whatever is clearly and distinctly perceived is true.

Descartes does, as a matter of fact, believe that all the steps in the proof of God's existence can be clearly and distinctly perceived at once.[2] It is plausible to suppose that he also thinks it possible to perceive simultaneously not only these steps but also the further steps involved in arguing that the truth of whatever is perceived clearly and distinctly is guaranteed by the existence of God. Without begging any questions or in any way committing the fallacy of circularity, then, Descartes allows the possibility of our being certain that whatever we clearly and distinctly perceive is true. For our belief in this principle may be rooted in present perceptions so that we are incapable of doubting it no matter what else we know or believe.

But this hardly settles the question of whether Descartes argues in a circle. What it shows is merely that without relying upon a circular argument it is possible to be certain that whatever is clearly and distinctly perceived is true. To attain this certainty one need only run through the argument that God exists and validates reason, keeping all relevant perceptions in mind at once. Being certain

---

[1] HR II, 92; AT VII, 214, ll. 8-14.
[2] Charles Adam, ed., *Entretien avec Burman* (Paris: Boivin, 1937), pp. 9-13; AT V, 148-149.

171

of the principle that what is clearly and distinctly perceived is true, however, is not the same as knowing it to be true. And it would seem that this principle, like other objects of clear and distinct perception, can well be doubted when one is not perceiving it but only remembering that it has been perceived.

The remarkable thing is that Descartes denies this. He asserts quite straightforwardly that after it has once been demonstrated that what is clearly and distinctly perceived is true, one need not run through all the perceptions comprising this demonstration each time that it is necessary to invoke the divine guarantee. Here is what he says:

> *After I have perceived that there is a God . . . and from that have concluded that all those things that I perceive clearly and distinctly are necessarily true, then, even if I attend no further to the reasons for which I judged that this was true, just as long as I recall that I did perceive clearly and distinctly, no contrary reason can be brought forward that could drive me to doubt; rather, I have true and certain knowledge of it.*[3]

When a person wishes to invoke the principle that what is clearly and distinctly perceived is true, Descartes asserts, it is sufficient for him to remember having demonstrated it. It is not necessary for him to repeat the perceptions that comprise its demonstration.

But why not? Why should this principle be established by the recollection that it was once demonstrated when, in general, recalling that something has been perceived clearly and distinctly is not sufficient to establish it? Does it not surely seem that Descartes is guilty here of an egregious fallacy? For does he not sanction accepting as evidence for the principle that clear and distinct perceptions are true the fact that this principle was once perceived clearly and distinctly? And does not accepting such evidence for the principle simply beg the entire question—the question, precisely, of whether such evidence is acceptable?

Before answering these questions it will be useful to examine carefully the last passage quoted, in which Descartes explains how things stand when the existence of God has once been demonstrated and when it has once been seen clearly and distinctly that from God's existence it follows that what is clearly and distinctly perceived is true. Notice what he claims to be the case when he recollects having perceived that God guarantees the truth of what

[3] HR I, 184; AT VII, 70.

is clearly and distinctly perceived. He claims that then "no contrary reason can be brought forward that could drive me to doubt." He does not assert that when he recollects having perceived that his principle of evidence is true he cannot then *experience* doubts as to its truth. Nor does he deny what is in any case surely not deniable —that he can always *state* that he doubts it. His point is rather that any such statement will be logically capricious: he cannot, Descartes claims, *have a reason* for the doubt.

Now Descartes does, of course, regard the possibility that there is not a veracious God as a reason for doubting that whatever is clearly and distinctly perceived is true. So his claim means that when a person remembers both that he once perceived God's existence and that he also once perceived that what is clearly and distinctly perceived is true, it is not then reasonable for him to entertain the possibility that a veracious God does not exist. But why is it unreasonable, when we may doubt other things that we recall having perceived clearly and distinctly?

Consider just what it is that is being recalled in the case at issue —namely, that exercising reason in the most rigorous way results in the clear and distinct perception that a veracious God exists. When reason is used in the most impeccable manner, the conclusion to which it leads excludes the possibility that there is an omnipotent demon; indeed, it excludes the possibility that man's being derives from a source that is in any way defective in power or in perfection. Descartes has undertaken to show that *reason provides no basis for doubting what is clearly and distinctly perceived*, and it is the establishment of this conclusion that is recalled.

Far from leading to the discovery of reasons for mistrusting reason, Descartes attempts to show, the most conscientious use of reason leads to the discovery that such mistrust has no rational ground. When someone remembers having perceived clearly and distinctly that reason is guaranteed by God, he remembers in effect that there is no good reason for doubting the trustworthiness of reason. What he remembers is, in other words, that the metaphysical doubt is utterly capricious. It is readily apparent in the following passage that Descartes regards this as sufficient to establish the truth of what is clearly and distinctly perceived:

> *After it is known that God exists, it is necessary to imagine that he is a deceiver if we want to cast doubt again on the things we perceive clearly and distinctly. And since one cannot imagine that*

173

He is a deceiver, these things must be altogether admitted as true and certain.[4]

The second of these sentences reveals the "negative" character of Descartes's procedure. He establishes truths by removing the grounds for doubting them rather than by proving their truth in a direct way. This is, of course, quite consistent with the fact that his most fundamental preoccupation is to find beliefs that are "solid and permanent." It suggests that his most basic criterion for the acceptability of a belief is indubitability and that his conception of truth is to be understood in terms of this criterion.

Since my purpose here is not to decide whether Descartes actually succeeds in validating reason, but only to clarify the nature of his undertaking, it is outside the scope of this discussion to examine the proof of God's existence that plays a central role in his argument. I wish briefly to point out, however, that his "causal proof" is one of the most strikingly Platonic elements of his thought. It is quite similar, in fact, to an argument that Socrates uses to establish his theory of recollection.[5] Socrates argues that our descriptions of the world of sensory experience necessarily involve the use of ideal standards and that our possession of these standards cannot originate in sensory experience; knowledge of the ideal must therefore be innate, he maintains; it derives, on his account, from a non-sensory encounter with the ideal itself. Descartes argues similarly that he could not recognize his own imperfection, as in fact he does, unless he had an idea of perfection; and since he finds no perfection in his experience, this idea must be innate and must originate in some kind of encounter with what is itself perfect. The thrust of both arguments is to show that knowledge of the ideal is prior to —i.e., is presupposed by—knowledge of what is actual; and that it can only be derived, therefore, directly from the ideal itself.

How Descartes's reasoning about reason is to be understood becomes clearer when account is taken of the general nature of his enterprise in the *Meditations*. He is largely concerned with the problem of skepticism. Now as far as skepticism with regard to reason is concerned, the classical gambit of the skeptic is to show that the use of reason leads ineluctably to the conclusion that reason is unreliable. Indeed this is, apart from a stubborn and mindless cynicism, the skeptic's only available gambit. If he is to argue at all, and not just content himself with inconsequential mockery,

[4] HR II, 141; AT VII, 144, ll. 16-20.
[5] *Phaedo* 74d-75b.

he can only attempt to *demonstrate* the untrustworthiness of reason. Naturally this attempt cannot succeed unless his arguments are good ones, i.e., unless he can give good reasons for being suspicious of the value of good reasons. The philosophical skeptic must show that reason can be turned against itself by showing that there are reasons of the very strongest sort for doubting its reliability. His arguments must be designed, in other words, to provide a *reductio ad absurdum* of the assumption that reason is reliable.

In order to dispose of skepticism with regard to reason, therefore, it is only necessary to show that the skeptic's attempt to overthrow reason fails. Descartes believes he can accomplish this by making it clear that the most rigorous use of reason does not lead to a mistrust of reason but, rather, to conclusions excluding all basis for such mistrust. Descartes takes his task to be precisely to show that the skeptic's *reductio* argument cannot be generated. He attempts this by offering a proof that there is an omnipotent deity who is not a deceiver and whose existence entails that reason is reliable. The value of the proof depends upon its success in showing where the right use of reason in fact leads: to wit, neither to the conclusion that there is an omnipotent demon devoted to deception, nor to any other conclusion involving the untrustworthiness of reason. The proof purports to reveal that when reason is put to proper use it produces reasons of the very best sort (i.e., clear and distinct perceptions) for trusting reason. It produces no such reasons for mistrusting reason, and this means that the skeptic's attempt to reduce reliance on reason to absurdity fails.

Descartes's argument, then, is an attempt to show that there are no good reasons for believing that reason is unreliable—that the mistrust of reason is not supported by reason and that it is accordingly irrational. The proof that God exists precludes the existence of a demon and therefore entails that the demon hypothesis is not a good reason for doubt. There cannot be two omnipotent beings; if God exists, there can be no demon. Descartes comes to recognize, moreover, that the demon hypothesis is not itself coherent. Infinite power entails infinite goodness, he observes, and the notion of an omnipotent being who is evil is not an intelligible one. The demon hypothesis turns out to be self-contradictory and thus it cannot serve as a good reason for skepticism.

The import of the proof of God's existence is very general. It eliminates not only the demon hypothesis but *every* hypothesis that might serve as a basis for mistrusting reason. If man's nature derives from a perfect being then his nature can have no inherent and inescapable defects whatever. Men would be unable to escape deception if reason were inherently defective, for they have no faculty superior to reason. It is clear that God has not protected men entirely from the commission of error, but it would be inconsistent with His nature to have made a creature incapable of correcting its mistakes. Human reason may be weak and imperfect, but it cannot be intrinsically untrustworthy or inescapably misleading.

The point of Descartes's validation of reason is that if reason is properly employed—that is, if we give assent only to what we clearly and distinctly perceive—we are not led to doubt that reason is reliable. We are led, on the contrary, to assent to the propositions that God exists and that He guarantees the reliability of reason. As long as the existence of an omnipotent demon had to be acknowledged as a possibility, Descartes had to acknowledge that the use of reason might lead to the verification of this hypothesis, and this to the conclusion that reason is not reliable. The crux of Descartes's validation of reason is not so much the discovery that a benign deity exists, but that reason leads to the conclusion that such a deity exists. Since the proof of God's existence eliminates not only the demon hypothesis but every hypothesis that might serve as a basis for mistrusting reason, its value is in effect a proof of the consistency of reason, i.e., a proof that no set of clear and distinct perceptions can be self-contradictory. For it shows that no proposition entailing the unreliability of reason can be clearly and distinctly perceived.

Suppose a person recalls having perceived something clearly and distinctly and wonders if he is entitled to regard what he perceived as certainly true. If he does not know whether the skeptic can succeed in the attempt to provide a *reductio ad absurdum* of the trustworthiness of reason, then he must properly be uncertain whether whatever is perceived clearly and distinctly is true. For all he knows, it may be possible to find impeccable grounds for regarding reason as unreliable—for example, by showing clearly and distinctly that there is an omnipotent demon bent on spoiling the work of reason. And as long as this possibility remains, he must fear that he may subsequently perceive clearly and distinctly something that is inconsistent with what he has already clearly and distinctly perceived. But such doubts are legitimately dispelled, Descartes maintains, if the person can recall that the existence of a veracious God has been demonstrated. For he then recalls that reason does not fall victim to the skeptic's *reductio* but that it decisively escapes this danger. That the existence of a veracious God has been clearly and distinctly perceived answers the question concerning the possible success of the skeptic's line of argument. It means that the skeptic's argument fails. This question being answered, there remain no reasonable grounds upon which to base metaphysical doubts.

It is evident that Descartes's argument does not suffer from the commonly charged circularity. Metaphysical doubt concerns the truth of what is clearly and distinctly perceived, and the removal of this doubt is effected without assuming that what is clearly and distinctly perceived is true. It is removed simply by the knowledge that a certain demonstration has been successfully accomplished. This knowledge is, of course, that certain things have been clearly and distinctly perceived. But that the *truth* of these things be supposed is not required, and so the question is not begged. All that is relevant to the removal of metaphysical doubt is that the skeptic's *reductio* be discovered not to materialize and this discovery can be made and recalled without anything clearly and distinctly perceived being supposed to be true.

This does not mean, however that Descartes's reasoning is free of defect. It does not even mean that it is free of circularity. Descartes seems to have overlooked the following embarrassing question: Given that reason leads to the conclusion that reason is reliable because a veracious God exists, may it not also lead to the conclusion that there is an omnipotent demon whose existence renders reason unreliable? These two conclusions are incompatible, to be sure, and if the proper use of reason established both of them, this would mean that reason is not reliable. But Descartes cannot simply take it for granted that this is not the case. His procedure does seem to beg the question, therefore, although it does so in a rather different way than has generally been thought. Descartes attempts to provide what amounts to a proof of the consistency of reason. But his proof appears to be decisive only if one assumes, thereby apparently begging the question, that reason is in fact consistent. For otherwise it might still be possible to construct an equally cogent proof of the inconsistency of reason.

Perhaps it is only to be expected that Descartes's validation of reason will break down in some such way as this. But it is worth noticing that its breakdown is not of merely parochial interest. In attempting to show that clear and distinct perceptions are consistent, Descartes confronts a problem that must be confronted by any serious theory of knowledge. It is difficult to see how any "solution" of this problem could go further than his. All reasoning involves a reliance, as Descartes insists, on "clear and distinct perceptions"— that is, on perceptions so elementary and indispensable that it is impossible either to do without them or to reduce them to others less difficult. How does a person know, for instance, that a certain simple argument is of the form *modus ponens?* He looks at it, thinks about it, perhaps sets it beside a formal expression; in the end, he must just see that it does have that form. And what if he looks and thinks and compares again, and this time sees just as clearly that it does not? In such an event, I suppose, he would search initially for circumstances in the one case or the other that might explain the discrepancy. But suppose he cannot find them; suppose both perceptions occurred under ideal conditions. Then his conclusion might perhaps be that reason is unreliable and that even its best testimony cannot be trusted to stand up. To draw this conclusion would be to acknowledge that the proposition that reason is reliable is a contingent one and might be false. This seems to be the possibility that haunts Descartes and that he attempts to refute by proving that a trustworthy deity exists. In effect he offers an a priori proof of a proposition that he takes, at least initially, to be empirical and contingent.

There is another way to handle the problem. One could begin by refusing to admit the possibility that reason is untrustworthy and treat its reliability as something to which no contingencies are relevant. This involves denying that two inconsistent perceptions can both occur under equally ideal conditions, that is, denying that any inconsistency can arise between perceptions that are really clear and distinct. Whenever a discrepancy between perceptions seems to occur, then, one would insist that at least one of the perceptions must have occurred under less than ideal conditions; and one would persist in this even if it meant radically reinterpreting one's experience in order to avoid the admission that the two perceptions were equally clear and distinct. This approach to the problem of the reliability of reason is more congenial to the contemporary philosophical mind than the one Descartes chose. Whether it is superior to his approach is a large question, concerning which I shall say nothing here.

I have attempted to show that Descartes's reasoning in the *Meditations* is designed not so much to prove that what is clearly and distinctly perceived is true, as to establish that there are no reasona-

ble grounds for doubting this. It might be objected that this interpretation entails that Descartes leaves the main question still open.
For why may it not be the case that what we clearly and distinctly
perceive is sometimes false even if we can have no reasonable
grounds for supposing so? If this objection has any weight at all, it
bears against Descartes's doctrines themselves and not against the
authenticity of my interpretation of them. My interpretation receives some confirmation, indeed, from the fact that Descartes
acknowledges that an objection of this sort may well be raised
against his views.

One of his summary statements of his position begins with the
assertion: "if . . . we can never have any cause to be in doubt about
what we have thus persuaded ourselves of, there is nothing more
for us to seek; we have all that one may reasonably wish."[6] Immediately thereafter he anticipates the objection that certainty based
upon the unavailability of reasonable grounds for doubt is compatible with the falsity of what one is certain of. It is particularly
interesting to consider his manner of formulating this objection and
of responding to it. Concerning something of which we have all the
certainty that "one may reasonably wish," he says:

> *What is it to us if someone should perhaps imagine that the
> very thing of whose truth we have been so firmly persuaded ap-
> pears false to God or to an angel and that as a consequence it is
> false speaking absolutely? What do we care about this absolute
> falsity, since we by no means believe in it or even have the least
> suspicion of it? For we are supposing a persuasion so firm that
> it can in no way be removed—a persuasion, therefore, that is
> exactly the same as the most perfect certainty.*[7]

Descartes evidently recognizes that his position entails that from
our knowing something with perfect certitude it does not follow
that it is, "speaking absolutely," true. He explicitly concedes, in
other words, that he has not proven that whatever is clearly and
distinctly perceived is "absolutely" true.

What he suggests is that if something that is perfectly certain may
be absolutely false, then the notions of absolute truth and absolute
falsity are irrelevant to the purposes of inquiry. His account makes
it clear that the notion of truth that *is* relevant is a notion of
coherence. Descartes cares less about the correspondence of his
beliefs to "reality" than he does about their permanence and con-

---

[6] HR II, 41; AT VII, 144, l. 28—145, l. 1.
[7] AT VII, 145, ll. 1-8.

stancy. What he wishes above all to avoid is not error, in the sense of non-correspondence, but betrayal. What might be *found out* to be false is what he wishes to guard against. If a belief can confidently be expected to remain unshaken by any further inquiry, that is all the truth he cares to demand.

TRUTH AND REALITY: THE GALILEO CONTROVERSY

I wish now to present a theory about the *Meditations* that is even more speculative than those developed above. The theory is both plausible and interesting, I believe, but unfortunately I am unable to provide any direct evidence for it. Perhaps such evidence exists, or perhaps there exists good evidence that the theory is false. Since neither kind of evidence is known to me, I shall simply describe the theory briefly and explain why I find it plausible.

During Descartes's lifetime there was a famous controversy between Galileo and the Catholic Church over the Copernican theory of the solar system. This controversy is widely supposed to have been due essentially to an obscurantist attempt on the part of a reactionary institution to defend the inviolability of biblical revelation against the incursions of rational scientific inquiry. No doubt there were many silly people on both sides of the dispute, preoccupied with a variety of issues of greater and lesser intrinsic seriousness. But there was, among the questions disputed, at least one of great philosophical difficulty and importance. In a somewhat different form, this question is still very much in contention among philosophers today. And, at least up to a point, the Church's position on this question was quite a bit stronger and more "modern" than Galileo's.

In a letter written in 1615, long before the Church finally required Galileo to recant his views, Cardinal Bellarmine indicated the basic philosophical point at issue. Bellarmine's letter is addressed to Paolo Antonio Foscarini, a Carmelite monk from Naples, who was a partisan of Galileo's doctrine. It includes the following statements:

> *It seems to me that your Reverence and Signor Galileo act prudently when you content yourselves with speaking hypothetically and not absolutely, as I have always understood that Coper-*

nicus spoke. To say that on the supposition of the Earth's move-
ment and the Sun's quiescence all the celestial appearances are
explained better than by the theory of eccentrics and epicycles is
to speak with excellent good sense and to run no risk whatever.
Such a manner of speaking is enough for a mathematician. But
to want to affirm that the Sun, in very truth, is at the center of
the universe and only rotates on its axis without going from east
to west, is a very dangerous attitude. . . . If there were a real proof
that the Sun is in the center of the universe, that the Earth is in
the third heaven, and that the Sun does not go round the Earth
but the Earth round the Sun, then we should have to proceed with
great circumspection in explaining passages of Scripture which
appear to teach the contrary, and rather admit that we did not
understand them than declare an opinion to be false which is
proved to be true. But, as for myself, I shall not believe that there
are such proofs until they are shown to me. Nor is it proof that,
if the Sun be supposed at the center of the universe and the Earth
in the third heaven, everything works out the same as if it were
the other way around. In case of doubt we ought not to abandon
the interpretation of the sacred text. . . .[1]

The Church's position, as Bellarmine presents it, is not a simple
insistence that the authority of sacred texts must be honored come
what may. If there should be a *proof* that some passage in the
Bible is literally false, the Church will acknowledge the necessity
of reinterpreting the passage. But the fact that heliocentrism saves
the appearances "better" than does the geocentric theory is not
conclusive evidence that heliocentrism is true. In the absence of
such evidence, revelation takes precedence over what appeals to
the scientific mind.

If both the geocentric and the heliocentric theories are equally
capable of accommodating all relevant empirical data—that is, if
each succeeds in saving all the appearances—then, according to the
Church, either theory might be true. God might have chosen either
a geocentric or a heliocentric design for the solar system; indeed,
he might have chosen *any* design consistent with the empirical
data. The question is: How are we to decide which alternative God
actually chose?

Now except for the reference to God, this analysis of the problem
of establishing scientific theories is widely current today. It is frequently held nowadays that any body of empirical data may be

[1] Quoted in Giorgio de Santillana, *The Crime of Galileo* (Chicago: University of
Chicago Press, 1955), pp. 98-100.

accommodated by a variety of theories, and that no theory can therefore be satisfactorily established on empirical grounds alone. It is no longer customary to ask how we are to decide which of these alternative theories corresponds to God's design of the universe, but rather simply to wonder how to justify the selection of one among the alternatives as "true."

The Church maintained, rather plausibly, that there is no way to know which logically possible alternative God chose unless he tells us. But since God in fact wrote a Book in which he explained what he had done, the difficulty is not insuperable: this book provides a basis for making decisions when the data are equivocal. The most popular modern view is that the selection among alternative theories is to be made on "pragmatic" grounds. The exact nature of these grounds is generally not much clearer than the "real" meaning of a Biblical text, but they are generally said to include such considerations as "simplicity" and "convenience."

In any event, modern pragmatists and the seventeenth-century Church agree that questions of scientific truth cannot be decided on the basis of empirical evidence alone. They differ, however, in their metaphysics. The Church understands a true theory to be one that reflects the independent character of reality; a true theory describes the world as God made it. On the pragmatists' account, to say that a theory is true is to say just that it is the simplest, etc., of the various alternatives that successfully accommodate the relevant data. Many pragmatists would be inclined to deny that there is any serious meaning in the question of whether the world "really" is like the description provided by the pragmatically most acceptable theory. The notion of an independent reality, which serves as a control and a goal in the selection of theories, tends to disappear in pragmatism.

Seen in this light, it is clear that the dispute between Galileo and the Church involved very significant issues concerning the relation between thought and reality and the nature of scientific truth. Now it is extremely difficult to believe that Descartes ignored these issues. He was deeply preoccupied with the philosophical foundations of scientific inquiry, and could not have been indifferent to the very fundamental problems at issue in the Galileo affair. He must have felt the necessity of coming to terms with them—no serious philosopher with his interests could have failed to do so. Yet the curious and tantalizing fact is that Descartes never comes out and says what stand he takes in the controversy.

This is, in a sense, easy enough to understand. Descartes was a cautious man and had good reason to wish to avoid becoming embroiled. Considerations of prudence may sufficiently account for his failure to enter the controversy in an explicit and conspicuous way. But they cannot account for a refusal on his part to adopt a position for himself, for the questions involved were too crucial and too germane to his enterprise. Even if he chose not to publicize his stand, he must have taken one in his own mind. He must have had a solution to the problem raised by the Church in its attack on Galileo.

What, then, is his solution, and where is it to be found? Although Descartes does not identify the work as such, it seems to me that the *Meditations* is in fact largely devoted to an attempt on his part to develop a position on the issues disputed by Galileo and the Church. These issues involved the relation between human reason and reality and the possibility of man's attaining a knowledge corresponding to God's truth. These are precisely the issues involved in Descartes's attempt to validate reason. Descartes explores the epistemological implications of the dependence of human reason on God, and in doing so confronts the very same configuration of problems that exercised Galileo and the Church.

In his response to these problems, Descartes adopts neither the position of the Church nor that of Galileo. His alternative neatly avoids the point of contention between them and makes it unnecessary for him to deny the autonomy either of science or of revelation. Galileo and the Church fought because each claimed special access to the nature of things. The Church insisted that only God's word could authoritatively reveal the design of the world, at least wherever alternate designs were possible, while Galileo maintained that this design could be discovered by the use of natural reason in scientific inquiry. Descartes, on the other hand, leaves God's truth to God and claims for science only a truth sufficient for man.

Reason, he argues, can give us certainty. It can serve to establish beliefs in which there is no risk of betrayal. This certainty is all we need and all we should demand. Perhaps our certainties do not coincide with God's truth; they may not describe the world as it looks to a divine intelligence. But this divine or absolute truth, since it is outside the range of our faculties and cannot undermine our certainties, need be of no concern to us. There are, if you like, two truths. One is a reflection of the nature of the world as it appears to God—absolute, free of the perspective that results when reality is approached from a particular and limited point of view. The other is cut to the measure of human reason and men can be secure with it. The absolute falsity of the latter, if it should be absolutely false, cannot become apparent to human reason and therefore need not be a matter of human concern. It may not grasp the inherent and absolute nature of reality, but it gives us all we need—beliefs upon which we can establish something "solid and permanent in the sciences."

I have said that there is no evidence that Descartes intended the views he develops in the *Meditations* as a solution of the conflict between Galileo and the Church. There is not even any evidence, so far as I am aware, that Descartes knew exactly what issues were involved in this conflict. It seems likely that he did. He was generally very well informed and, even during his years of seclusion, kept in touch with intellectual affairs through correspondence with his friend Mersenne and others. Even if he did not know of Bellarmine's letter to Forscarini or of similar documents, it would not have been difficult for him to imagine what was at stake in the collision between science and religion in his time.

But suppose we refuse to guess what Descartes must have known and what he must have had in mind. Suppose we decline to read the *Meditations* as an attempt on his part to come to terms with the problems at issue between Galileo and the Church. At the very least we can still say that his book does include a possible solution to those problems. Whether he intended it or not, Descartes provides a way of dealing with the most urgent and explosive philosophical problem that arose as modern science sought to affirm its autonomy. His solution of it, as I have explained it, has a Kantian flavor: men may content themselves with certainty about phenomena and leave the noumenon to God. I do not wish to press or explore the analogy between his views and those of Kant. It should be no surprise, however, that the approach Descartes took in his metaphysical attempt to create the foundations of science should be developed by other great philosophers in an era of continual philosophical preoccupation with the existence as well as the results of the sciences. Nor is it a surprise that the first great modern philosopher should have had something important to say, whether intentionally or not, about the first great philosophical problem of the modern era.

Index

Index

God (*continued*)
  reliability of memory and, 160–162
  simple elements and, 70–72
  validating reason and, 156–58
    circularity, 158–60
Gouhier, Henri, 65*n*, 85–86
Gueroult, Martial, 56, 58, 65*n*

Habits, overcoming of, 14–15
Haldane, E. S., 63–64
Hardy, G. H., 150–51
Hintikka, Jaakko, 92*n*
Hobbes, Thomas, 14, 148
Human mind
  existence and, 81–84
  nature of, 98
  origin of, 81–84
Hume, David, 70–71

"I," 93, 106, 126–27
  body and, 122–23
  distinctness of perception of, 115–16
  sum and, 119–22, 133, 138–39
  See also Sum
Ideally qualified observers, 36, 39, 42
Ideas, 132–33
Imagination
  dreams and, 54–57, 69
  overthrow of beliefs and, 57–58
Impressions, 71
Inconsistencies, logical. *See* Logic, laws of
Indubitable, relationship between truth and, 162–66
Intuition, role of in reasoning
  in modern philosophy, 153–54
  in Second Meditation, 152–55

Judgments, 144
  basis of, 33–34
  guided by reason, 28
  madness and, 36–40, 82–83

  mathematical, 73
  memory and, 77
  suspension of, 16–18, 27
  truth of, 23, 44–45, 82

Kant, Immanuel, 185
Knowledge, adequate, 142–44
Koyré, Alexander, 3

Laporte, Jean, 58, 164*n*
Logic, laws of, 27, 33, 98, 121, 133–34, 153–54
  doubt of, 48
  God and, 7
  modus ponens, 152, 178
  reason and, 28
  reductio ad absurdum, 15, 51, 100, 175–76

Madness, effects upon judgment of, 36–40, 82–83
Malin génie. See Demon
Man
  definition of, 118–19
  essence of
    body, 122–23
    reason, 175–76
    soul, 119
    sum res cogitans, 117–19, 121–23
Material truth-values, 129, 162, 164, 167
Material world, existence of, 15, 69–71
Mathematics, 69, 85
  God and, 72
  judgments of, 73
  metaphysics and, 66–67
  overthrow of beliefs and, 16–17
  senses and, 61, 64–67, 73
  truth-value of, 73–78
Meditation as philosophic form
  Descartes's use of, 3–4
  religious, 4
Memory
  doubt and, 60–62